C-201 CAREER EXAMINATION SERIES

This is your
PASSBOOK for...

Foreman Water Distribution

Test Preparation Study Guide
Questions & Answers

NATIONAL LEARNING CORPORATION®

COPYRIGHT NOTICE

This book is SOLELY intended for, is sold ONLY to, and its use is RESTRICTED to individual, bona fide applicants or candidates who qualify by virtue of having seriously filed applications for appropriate license, certificate, professional and/or promotional advancement, higher school matriculation, scholarship, or other legitimate requirements of education and/or governmental authorities.

This book is NOT intended for use, class instruction, tutoring, training, duplication, copying, reprinting, excerption, or adaptation, etc., by:

1) Other publishers
2) Proprietors and/or Instructors of "Coaching" and/or Preparatory Courses
3) Personnel and/or Training Divisions of commercial, industrial, and governmental organizations
4) Schools, colleges, or universities and/or their departments and staffs, including teachers and other personnel
5) Testing Agencies or Bureaus
6) Study groups which seek by the purchase of a single volume to copy and/or duplicate and/or adapt this material for use by the group as a whole without having purchased individual volumes for each of the members of the group
7) Et al.

Such persons would be in violation of appropriate Federal and State statutes.

PROVISION OF LICENSING AGREEMENTS – Recognized educational, commercial, industrial, and governmental institutions and organizations, and others legitimately engaged in educational pursuits, including training, testing, and measurement activities, may address request for a licensing agreement to the copyright owners, who will determine whether, and under what conditions, including fees and charges, the materials in this book may be used them. In other words, a licensing facility exists for the legitimate use of the material in this book on other than an individual basis. However, it is asseverated and affirmed here that the material in this book CANNOT be used without the receipt of the express permission of such a licensing agreement from the Publishers. Inquiries re licensing should be addressed to the company, attention rights and permissions department.

All rights reserved, including the right of reproduction in whole or in part, in any form or by any means, electronic or mechanical, including photocopying, recording, or by any information storage and retrieval system, without permission in writing from the Publisher.

Copyright © 2025 by
National Learning Corporation

212 Michael Drive, Syosset, NY 11791
(516) 921-8888 • www.passbooks.com
E-mail: info@passbooks.com

PASSBOOK® SERIES

THE *PASSBOOK® SERIES* has been created to prepare applicants and candidates for the ultimate academic battlefield – the examination room.

At some time in our lives, each and every one of us may be required to take an examination – for validation, matriculation, admission, qualification, registration, certification, or licensure.

Based on the assumption that every applicant or candidate has met the basic formal educational standards, has taken the required number of courses, and read the necessary texts, the *PASSBOOK® SERIES* furnishes the one special preparation which may assure passing with confidence, instead of failing with insecurity. Examination questions – together with answers – are furnished as the basic vehicle for study so that the mysteries of the examination and its compounding difficulties may be eliminated or diminished by a sure method.

This book is meant to help you pass your examination provided that you qualify and are serious in your objective.

The entire field is reviewed through the huge store of content information which is succinctly presented through a provocative and challenging approach – the question-and-answer method.

A climate of success is established by furnishing the correct answers at the end of each test.

You soon learn to recognize types of questions, forms of questions, and patterns of questioning. You may even begin to anticipate expected outcomes.

You perceive that many questions are repeated or adapted so that you can gain acute insights, which may enable you to score many sure points.

You learn how to confront new questions, or types of questions, and to attack them confidently and work out the correct answers.

You note objectives and emphases, and recognize pitfalls and dangers, so that you may make positive educational adjustments.

Moreover, you are kept fully informed in relation to new concepts, methods, practices, and directions in the field.

You discover that you are actually taking the examination all the time: you are preparing for the examination by "taking" an examination, not by reading extraneous and/or supererogatory textbooks.

In short, this PASSBOOK®, used directedly, should be an important factor in helping you to pass your test.

FOREMAN (Water Distribution)

Foreman Water Distribution Division oversees the work of staff involved in the construction, maintenance, and repair of the water distribution system. A Utility Foreman in the Wastewater Collection Division oversees the work of staff involved in a sanitary sewer preventive maintenance program providing TV inspection, cleaning, repair and construction of the wastewater collection system; or staff performing blue stake locating. Supervision is exercised over any combination of Senior Utility Technicians, Utility Technicians/Trainees, Backhoe Operators, Equipment Operators, Utility TV Technicians, and/or Utility Specialty Technicians. Utility Foremen are subject to periodic rotation and are expected to be able to perform effectively in any of the assigned areas within their respective divisions. Work is performed under the general supervision of a Utility Supervisor or Senior Utility Supervisor who reviews the work by making work site visits and analyzing job reports.

ESSENTIAL FUNCTIONS:
- Monitors and directs crew activities to ensure safety and water quality or other policies are followed;
- Represents the City to citizens in resolving service requests and complaints and contacts property owners, contractors, utility company employees, and other City departments to coordinate the completion of service requests or to resolve problems;
- Coordinates the daily use of equipment;
- Coordinates activities with other departments, divisions, and sections to accomplish work tasks;
- Enforces safety regulations and directs barricading and traffic control when needed;
- Prepares investigative reports of accident, injury, and flood damage incidents;
- Calls or electronically generates requests for blue stake markings before construction projects begin;
- Maintains radio contact with all assigned staff and arranges for the delivery of materials and equipment to job sites;
- Pre-inspects job sites to determine the scope of work;
- Prepares field drawings of work performed;
- Maintains regular and reliable attendance.
- Demonstrates superior seamless customer service, integrity, and commitment to innovation, efficiency, and fiscally responsible activity.

Water Distribution:
- Supervises and evaluates the work of crews engaged in maintaining, monitoring, constructing, installing, replacing or repairing water mains and service lines of various sizes, or supervising crews engaged in specialty operations.

Wastewater Collection:
- Supervises and evaluates the work of employees engaged in the operation, maintenance, cleaning, inspection, preventive maintenance, repair and construction of the City's sanitary sewer system;
- Orders and accepts delivery of chemicals, equipment and materials while monitoring contractors.

Blue Stake:
- Supervises and evaluates the work of employees engaged in marking utilities including water and sewer infrastructure;
- Responds to damaged and unknown utilities to investigate and determine responsibility;
- Uses current information to determine locates for large or difficult projects.

Required Knowledge, Skills and Abilities:

Knowledge of:
- The general water distribution system or wastewater collection system.
- Methods, materials, tools and equipment used in constructing, maintaining, and repairing the water distribution system or in constructing, maintaining, repairing, and inspecting the wastewater collection system and related structures and facilities.
- Hazards of water distribution or wastewater collection work and safety measures to be observed, including trench safety, confined space entry, personal protective equipment hard hat, vest policies, and disinfection procedures.
- Construction techniques and sewer maintenance methods.
- Principles and practices of supervision.

Skill in:
- The use and care of equipment and tools used in constructing, maintaining, and repairing of the City's water distribution system or in constructing, maintaining, repairing, and inspecting of the City's wastewater collection system and related structures and facilities.

Ability to:
- Perform a broad range of supervisory responsibilities over others.
- Communicate orally with customers, clients or the public in either a face-to-face, one-to-one setting or by using a telephone.
- Observe or monitor objects or people's behavior to determine compliance with prescribed operating or safety standards.
- Comprehend and make inferences from written material, such as operations, maintenance and procedures manuals and Material Safety Data Sheets (MSDS).
- Read and interpret engineering specifications and drawings.
- Read and use graphic instructions such as quarter-section maps and other visual aids.
- Produce written documents with clearly organized thoughts using proper English sentence construction, punctuation, and grammar.
- Retrieve data or information from a terminal, PC, or other keyboard device on the service request system in order to plan and schedule work activities.
- Work in a variety of weather conditions with exposure to the elements.
- Learn job-related material through oral instruction and observation or through structured lecture and reading. This learning takes place in either an on-the-job training setting or in a classroom setting.
- Travel across rough, uneven, or rocky surfaces.
- Measure distance using a tape measure or other measuring device.
- Move heavy objects (50 pounds or more) short distances (20 feet or less).
- Work with raw sewage and chemicals in the collection system using only normal protective equipment (Wastewater Collection Division only).
- Work with disinfection and dechlorination chemicals in the distribution system using only normal protective equipment.
- Set up and remove barricades, traffic cones, or similar objects.
- Work safely without presenting a direct threat to self or others.

HOW TO TAKE A TEST

I. YOU MUST PASS AN EXAMINATION

A. WHAT EVERY CANDIDATE SHOULD KNOW
Examination applicants often ask us for help in preparing for the written test. What can I study in advance? What kinds of questions will be asked? How will the test be given? How will the papers be graded?

As an applicant for a civil service examination, you may be wondering about some of these things. Our purpose here is to suggest effective methods of advance study and to describe civil service examinations.

Your chances for success on this examination can be increased if you know how to prepare. Those "pre-examination jitters" can be reduced if you know what to expect. You can even experience an adventure in good citizenship if you know why civil service exams are given.

B. WHY ARE CIVIL SERVICE EXAMINATIONS GIVEN?
Civil service examinations are important to you in two ways. As a citizen, you want public jobs filled by employees who know how to do their work. As a job seeker, you want a fair chance to compete for that job on an equal footing with other candidates. The best-known means of accomplishing this two-fold goal is the competitive examination.

Exams are widely publicized throughout the nation. They may be administered for jobs in federal, state, city, municipal, town or village governments or agencies.

Any citizen may apply, with some limitations, such as the age or residence of applicants. Your experience and education may be reviewed to see whether you meet the requirements for the particular examination. When these requirements exist, they are reasonable and applied consistently to all applicants. Thus, a competitive examination may cause you some uneasiness now, but it is your privilege and safeguard.

C. HOW ARE CIVIL SERVICE EXAMS DEVELOPED?
Examinations are carefully written by trained technicians who are specialists in the field known as "psychological measurement," in consultation with recognized authorities in the field of work that the test will cover. These experts recommend the subject matter areas or skills to be tested; only those knowledges or skills important to your success on the job are included. The most reliable books and source materials available are used as references. Together, the experts and technicians judge the difficulty level of the questions.

Test technicians know how to phrase questions so that the problem is clearly stated. Their ethics do not permit "trick" or "catch" questions. Questions may have been tried out on sample groups, or subjected to statistical analysis, to determine their usefulness.

Written tests are often used in combination with performance tests, ratings of training and experience, and oral interviews. All of these measures combine to form the best-known means of finding the right person for the right job.

II. HOW TO PASS THE WRITTEN TEST

A. NATURE OF THE EXAMINATION

To prepare intelligently for civil service examinations, you should know how they differ from school examinations you have taken. In school you were assigned certain definite pages to read or subjects to cover. The examination questions were quite detailed and usually emphasized memory. Civil service exams, on the other hand, try to discover your present ability to perform the duties of a position, plus your potentiality to learn these duties. In other words, a civil service exam attempts to predict how successful you will be. Questions cover such a broad area that they cannot be as minute and detailed as school exam questions.

In the public service similar kinds of work, or positions, are grouped together in one "class." This process is known as *position-classification*. All the positions in a class are paid according to the salary range for that class. One class title covers all of these positions, and they are all tested by the same examination.

B. FOUR BASIC STEPS

1) Study the announcement

How, then, can you know what subjects to study? Our best answer is: "Learn as much as possible about the class of positions for which you've applied." The exam will test the knowledge, skills and abilities needed to do the work.

Your most valuable source of information about the position you want is the official exam announcement. This announcement lists the training and experience qualifications. Check these standards and apply only if you come reasonably close to meeting them.

The brief description of the position in the examination announcement offers some clues to the subjects which will be tested. Think about the job itself. Review the duties in your mind. Can you perform them, or are there some in which you are rusty? Fill in the blank spots in your preparation.

Many jurisdictions preview the written test in the exam announcement by including a section called "Knowledge and Abilities Required," "Scope of the Examination," or some similar heading. Here you will find out specifically what fields will be tested.

2) Review your own background

Once you learn in general what the position is all about, and what you need to know to do the work, ask yourself which subjects you already know fairly well and which need improvement. You may wonder whether to concentrate on improving your strong areas or on building some background in your fields of weakness. When the announcement has specified "some knowledge" or "considerable knowledge," or has used adjectives like "beginning principles of…" or "advanced … methods," you can get a clue as to the number and difficulty of questions to be asked in any given field. More questions, and hence broader coverage, would be included for those subjects which are more important in the work. Now weigh your strengths and weaknesses against the job requirements and prepare accordingly.

3) Determine the level of the position

Another way to tell how intensively you should prepare is to understand the level of the job for which you are applying. Is it the entering level? In other words, is this the position in which beginners in a field of work are hired? Or is it an intermediate or advanced level? Sometimes this is indicated by such words as "Junior" or "Senior" in the class title. Other jurisdictions use Roman numerals to designate the level – Clerk I, Clerk II, for example. The word "Supervisor" sometimes appears in the title. If the level is not indicated by the title, check the description of duties. Will you be working under very close supervision, or will you have responsibility for independent decisions in this work?

4) Choose appropriate study materials

Now that you know the subjects to be examined and the relative amount of each subject to be covered, you can choose suitable study materials. For beginning level jobs, or even advanced ones, if you have a pronounced weakness in some aspect of your training, read a modern, standard textbook in that field. Be sure it is up to date and has general coverage. Such books are normally available at your library, and the librarian will be glad to help you locate one. For entry-level positions, questions of appropriate difficulty are chosen – neither highly advanced questions, nor those too simple. Such questions require careful thought but not advanced training.

If the position for which you are applying is technical or advanced, you will read more advanced, specialized material. If you are already familiar with the basic principles of your field, elementary textbooks would waste your time. Concentrate on advanced textbooks and technical periodicals. Think through the concepts and review difficult problems in your field.

These are all general sources. You can get more ideas on your own initiative, following these leads. For example, training manuals and publications of the government agency which employs workers in your field can be useful, particularly for technical and professional positions. A letter or visit to the government department involved may result in more specific study suggestions, and certainly will provide you with a more definite idea of the exact nature of the position you are seeking.

III. KINDS OF TESTS

Tests are used for purposes other than measuring knowledge and ability to perform specified duties. For some positions, it is equally important to test ability to make adjustments to new situations or to profit from training. In others, basic mental abilities not dependent on information are essential. Questions which test these things may not appear as pertinent to the duties of the position as those which test for knowledge and information. Yet they are often highly important parts of a fair examination. For very general questions, it is almost impossible to help you direct your study efforts. What we can do is to point out some of the more common of these general abilities needed in public service positions and describe some typical questions.

1) General information

Broad, general information has been found useful for predicting job success in some kinds of work. This is tested in a variety of ways, from vocabulary lists to questions about current events. Basic background in some field of work, such as sociology or economics, may be sampled in a group of questions. Often these are principles which have become familiar to most persons through exposure rather than through formal training. It is difficult to advise you how to study for these questions; being alert to the world around you is our best suggestion.

2) Verbal ability

An example of an ability needed in many positions is verbal or language ability. Verbal ability is, in brief, the ability to use and understand words. Vocabulary and grammar tests are typical measures of this ability. Reading comprehension or paragraph interpretation questions are common in many kinds of civil service tests. You are given a paragraph of written material and asked to find its central meaning.

3) Numerical ability

Number skills can be tested by the familiar arithmetic problem, by checking paired lists of numbers to see which are alike and which are different, or by interpreting charts and graphs. In the latter test, a graph may be printed in the test booklet which you are asked to use as the basis for answering questions.

4) Observation

A popular test for law-enforcement positions is the observation test. A picture is shown to you for several minutes, then taken away. Questions about the picture test your ability to observe both details and larger elements.

5) Following directions

In many positions in the public service, the employee must be able to carry out written instructions dependably and accurately. You may be given a chart with several columns, each column listing a variety of information. The questions require you to carry out directions involving the information given in the chart.

6) Skills and aptitudes

Performance tests effectively measure some manual skills and aptitudes. When the skill is one in which you are trained, such as typing or shorthand, you can practice. These tests are often very much like those given in business school or high school courses. For many of the other skills and aptitudes, however, no short-time preparation can be made. Skills and abilities natural to you or that you have developed throughout your lifetime are being tested.

Many of the general questions just described provide all the data needed to answer the questions and ask you to use your reasoning ability to find the answers. Your best preparation for these tests, as well as for tests of facts and ideas, is to be at your physical and mental best. You, no doubt, have your own methods of getting into an exam-taking mood and keeping "in shape." The next section lists some ideas on this subject.

IV. KINDS OF QUESTIONS

Only rarely is the "essay" question, which you answer in narrative form, used in civil service tests. Civil service tests are usually of the short-answer type. Full instructions for answering these questions will be given to you at the examination. But in case this is your first experience with short-answer questions and separate answer sheets, here is what you need to know:

1) Multiple-choice Questions

Most popular of the short-answer questions is the "multiple choice" or "best answer" question. It can be used, for example, to test for factual knowledge, ability to solve problems or judgment in meeting situations found at work.

A multiple-choice question is normally one of three types—
- It can begin with an incomplete statement followed by several possible endings. You are to find the one ending which *best* completes the statement, although some of the others may not be entirely wrong.
- It can also be a complete statement in the form of a question which is answered by choosing one of the statements listed.

- It can be in the form of a problem – again you select the best answer.

Here is an example of a multiple-choice question with a discussion which should give you some clues as to the method for choosing the right answer:

When an employee has a complaint about his assignment, the action which will *best* help him overcome his difficulty is to
  A. discuss his difficulty with his coworkers
  B. take the problem to the head of the organization
  C. take the problem to the person who gave him the assignment
  D. say nothing to anyone about his complaint

In answering this question, you should study each of the choices to find which is best. Consider choice "A" – Certainly an employee may discuss his complaint with fellow employees, but no change or improvement can result, and the complaint remains unresolved. Choice "B" is a poor choice since the head of the organization probably does not know what assignment you have been given, and taking your problem to him is known as "going over the head" of the supervisor. The supervisor, or person who made the assignment, is the person who can clarify it or correct any injustice. Choice "C" is, therefore, correct. To say nothing, as in choice "D," is unwise. Supervisors have and interest in knowing the problems employees are facing, and the employee is seeking a solution to his problem.

2) True/False Questions

The "true/false" or "right/wrong" form of question is sometimes used. Here a complete statement is given. Your job is to decide whether the statement is right or wrong.

SAMPLE: A roaming cell-phone call to a nearby city costs less than a non-roaming call to a distant city.

This statement is wrong, or false, since roaming calls are more expensive.

This is not a complete list of all possible question forms, although most of the others are variations of these common types. You will always get complete directions for answering questions. Be sure you understand *how* to mark your answers – ask questions until you do.

V. RECORDING YOUR ANSWERS

Computer terminals are used more and more today for many different kinds of exams.
For an examination with very few applicants, you may be told to record your answers in the test booklet itself. Separate answer sheets are much more common. If this separate answer sheet is to be scored by machine – and this is often the case – it is highly important that you mark your answers correctly in order to get credit.
An electronic scoring machine is often used in civil service offices because of the speed with which papers can be scored. Machine-scored answer sheets must be marked with a pencil, which will be given to you. This pencil has a high graphite content which responds to the electronic scoring machine. As a matter of fact, stray dots may register as answers, so do not let your pencil rest on the answer sheet while you are pondering the correct answer. Also, if your pencil lead breaks or is otherwise defective, ask for another.

Since the answer sheet will be dropped in a slot in the scoring machine, be careful not to bend the corners or get the paper crumpled.

The answer sheet normally has five vertical columns of numbers, with 30 numbers to a column. These numbers correspond to the question numbers in your test booklet. After each number, going across the page are four or five pairs of dotted lines. These short dotted lines have small letters or numbers above them. The first two pairs may also have a "T" or "F" above the letters. This indicates that the first two pairs only are to be used if the questions are of the true-false type. If the questions are multiple choice, disregard the "T" and "F" and pay attention only to the small letters or numbers.

Answer your questions in the manner of the sample that follows:

32. The largest city in the United States is
    A. Washington, D.C.
    B. New York City
    C. Chicago
    D. Detroit
    E. San Francisco

1) Choose the answer you think is best. (New York City is the largest, so "B" is correct.)
2) Find the row of dotted lines numbered the same as the question you are answering. (Find row number 32)
3) Find the pair of dotted lines corresponding to the answer. (Find the pair of lines under the mark "B.")
4) Make a solid black mark between the dotted lines.

VI. BEFORE THE TEST

Common sense will help you find procedures to follow to get ready for an examination. Too many of us, however, overlook these sensible measures. Indeed, nervousness and fatigue have been found to be the most serious reasons why applicants fail to do their best on civil service tests. Here is a list of reminders:

- Begin your preparation early – Don't wait until the last minute to go scurrying around for books and materials or to find out what the position is all about.
- Prepare continuously – An hour a night for a week is better than an all-night cram session. This has been definitely established. What is more, a night a week for a month will return better dividends than crowding your study into a shorter period of time.
- Locate the place of the exam – You have been sent a notice telling you when and where to report for the examination. If the location is in a different town or otherwise unfamiliar to you, it would be well to inquire the best route and learn something about the building.
- Relax the night before the test – Allow your mind to rest. Do not study at all that night. Plan some mild recreation or diversion; then go to bed early and get a good night's sleep.
- Get up early enough to make a leisurely trip to the place for the test – This way unforeseen events, traffic snarls, unfamiliar buildings, etc. will not upset you.
- Dress comfortably – A written test is not a fashion show. You will be known by number and not by name, so wear something comfortable.

- Leave excess paraphernalia at home – Shopping bags and odd bundles will get in your way. You need bring only the items mentioned in the official notice you received; usually everything you need is provided. Do not bring reference books to the exam. They will only confuse those last minutes and be taken away from you when in the test room.
- Arrive somewhat ahead of time – If because of transportation schedules you must get there very early, bring a newspaper or magazine to take your mind off yourself while waiting.
- Locate the examination room – When you have found the proper room, you will be directed to the seat or part of the room where you will sit. Sometimes you are given a sheet of instructions to read while you are waiting. Do not fill out any forms until you are told to do so; just read them and be prepared.
- Relax and prepare to listen to the instructions
- If you have any physical problem that may keep you from doing your best, be sure to tell the test administrator. If you are sick or in poor health, you really cannot do your best on the exam. You can come back and take the test some other time.

VII. AT THE TEST

The day of the test is here and you have the test booklet in your hand. The temptation to get going is very strong. Caution! There is more to success than knowing the right answers. You must know how to identify your papers and understand variations in the type of short-answer question used in this particular examination. Follow these suggestions for maximum results from your efforts:

1) Cooperate with the monitor

The test administrator has a duty to create a situation in which you can be as much at ease as possible. He will give instructions, tell you when to begin, check to see that you are marking your answer sheet correctly, and so on. He is not there to guard you, although he will see that your competitors do not take unfair advantage. He wants to help you do your best.

2) Listen to all instructions

Don't jump the gun! Wait until you understand all directions. In most civil service tests you get more time than you need to answer the questions. So don't be in a hurry. Read each word of instructions until you clearly understand the meaning. Study the examples, listen to all announcements and follow directions. Ask questions if you do not understand what to do.

3) Identify your papers

Civil service exams are usually identified by number only. You will be assigned a number; you must not put your name on your test papers. Be sure to copy your number correctly. Since more than one exam may be given, copy your exact examination title.

4) Plan your time

Unless you are told that a test is a "speed" or "rate of work" test, speed itself is usually not important. Time enough to answer all the questions will be provided, but this does not mean that you have all day. An overall time limit has been set. Divide the total time (in minutes) by the number of questions to determine the approximate time you have for each question.

5) Do not linger over difficult questions

If you come across a difficult question, mark it with a paper clip (useful to have along) and come back to it when you have been through the booklet. One caution if you do this – be sure to skip a number on your answer sheet as well. Check often to be sure that you have not lost your place and that you are marking in the row numbered the same as the question you are answering.

6) Read the questions

Be sure you know what the question asks! Many capable people are unsuccessful because they failed to *read* the questions correctly.

7) Answer all questions

Unless you have been instructed that a penalty will be deducted for incorrect answers, it is better to guess than to omit a question.

8) Speed tests

It is often better NOT to guess on speed tests. It has been found that on timed tests people are tempted to spend the last few seconds before time is called in marking answers at random – without even reading them – in the hope of picking up a few extra points. To discourage this practice, the instructions may warn you that your score will be "corrected" for guessing. That is, a penalty will be applied. The incorrect answers will be deducted from the correct ones, or some other penalty formula will be used.

9) Review your answers

If you finish before time is called, go back to the questions you guessed or omitted to give them further thought. Review other answers if you have time.

10) Return your test materials

If you are ready to leave before others have finished or time is called, take ALL your materials to the monitor and leave quietly. Never take any test material with you. The monitor can discover whose papers are not complete, and taking a test booklet may be grounds for disqualification.

VIII. EXAMINATION TECHNIQUES

1) Read the general instructions carefully. These are usually printed on the first page of the exam booklet. As a rule, these instructions refer to the timing of the examination; the fact that you should not start work until the signal and must stop work at a signal, etc. If there are any *special* instructions, such as a choice of questions to be answered, make sure that you note this instruction carefully.

2) When you are ready to start work on the examination, that is as soon as the signal has been given, read the instructions to each question booklet, underline any key words or phrases, such as *least, best, outline, describe* and the like. In this way you will tend to answer as requested rather than discover on reviewing your paper that you *listed without describing*, that you selected the *worst* choice rather than the *best* choice, etc.

3) If the examination is of the objective or multiple-choice type – that is, each question will also give a series of possible answers: A, B, C or D, and you are called upon to select the best answer and write the letter next to that answer on your answer paper – it is advisable to start answering each question in turn. There may be anywhere from 50 to 100 such questions in the three or four hours allotted and you can see how much time would be taken if you read through all the questions before beginning to answer any. Furthermore, if you come across a question or group of questions which you know would be difficult to answer, it would undoubtedly affect your handling of all the other questions.

4) If the examination is of the essay type and contains but a few questions, it is a moot point as to whether you should read all the questions before starting to answer any one. Of course, if you are given a choice – say five out of seven and the like – then it is essential to read all the questions so you can eliminate the two that are most difficult. If, however, you are asked to answer all the questions, there may be danger in trying to answer the easiest one first because you may find that you will spend too much time on it. The best technique is to answer the first question, then proceed to the second, etc.

5) Time your answers. Before the exam begins, write down the time it started, then add the time allowed for the examination and write down the time it must be completed, then divide the time available somewhat as follows:
    - If 3-1/2 hours are allowed, that would be 210 minutes. If you have 80 objective-type questions, that would be an average of 2-1/2 minutes per question. Allow yourself no more than 2 minutes per question, or a total of 160 minutes, which will permit about 50 minutes to review.
    - If for the time allotment of 210 minutes there are 7 essay questions to answer, that would average about 30 minutes a question. Give yourself only 25 minutes per question so that you have about 35 minutes to review.

6) The most important instruction is to *read each question* and make sure you know what is wanted. The second most important instruction is to *time yourself properly* so that you answer every question. The third most important instruction is to *answer every question*. Guess if you have to but include something for each question. Remember that you will receive no credit for a blank and will probably receive some credit if you write something in answer to an essay question. If you guess a letter – say "B" for a multiple-choice question – you may have guessed right. If you leave a blank as an answer to a multiple-choice question, the examiners may respect your feelings but it will not add a point to your score. Some exams may penalize you for wrong answers, so in such cases *only*, you may not want to guess unless you have some basis for your answer.

7) Suggestions
    a. Objective-type questions
        1. Examine the question booklet for proper sequence of pages and questions
        2. Read all instructions carefully
        3. Skip any question which seems too difficult; return to it after all other questions have been answered
        4. Apportion your time properly; do not spend too much time on any single question or group of questions

5. Note and underline key words – *all, most, fewest, least, best, worst, same, opposite,* etc.
6. Pay particular attention to negatives
7. Note unusual option, e.g., unduly long, short, complex, different or similar in content to the body of the question
8. Observe the use of "hedging" words – *probably, may, most likely,* etc.
9. Make sure that your answer is put next to the same number as the question
10. Do not second-guess unless you have good reason to believe the second answer is definitely more correct
11. Cross out original answer if you decide another answer is more accurate; do not erase until you are ready to hand your paper in
12. Answer all questions; guess unless instructed otherwise
13. Leave time for review

   b. Essay questions
1. Read each question carefully
2. Determine exactly what is wanted. Underline key words or phrases.
3. Decide on outline or paragraph answer
4. Include many different points and elements unless asked to develop any one or two points or elements
5. Show impartiality by giving pros and cons unless directed to select one side only
6. Make and write down any assumptions you find necessary to answer the questions
7. Watch your English, grammar, punctuation and choice of words
8. Time your answers; don't crowd material

8) Answering the essay question

Most essay questions can be answered by framing the specific response around several key words or ideas. Here are a few such key words or ideas:

M's: manpower, materials, methods, money, management
P's: purpose, program, policy, plan, procedure, practice, problems, pitfalls, personnel, public relations

   a. Six basic steps in handling problems:
1. Preliminary plan and background development
2. Collect information, data and facts
3. Analyze and interpret information, data and facts
4. Analyze and develop solutions as well as make recommendations
5. Prepare report and sell recommendations
6. Install recommendations and follow up effectiveness

   b. Pitfalls to avoid
1. *Taking things for granted* – A statement of the situation does not necessarily imply that each of the elements is necessarily true; for example, a complaint may be invalid and biased so that all that can be taken for granted is that a complaint has been registered

2. *Considering only one side of a situation* – Wherever possible, indicate several alternatives and then point out the reasons you selected the best one
3. *Failing to indicate follow up* – Whenever your answer indicates action on your part, make certain that you will take proper follow-up action to see how successful your recommendations, procedures or actions turn out to be
4. *Taking too long in answering any single question* – Remember to time your answers properly

IX. AFTER THE TEST

Scoring procedures differ in detail among civil service jurisdictions although the general principles are the same. Whether the papers are hand-scored or graded by machine we have described, they are nearly always graded by number. That is, the person who marks the paper knows only the number – never the name – of the applicant. Not until all the papers have been graded will they be matched with names. If other tests, such as training and experience or oral interview ratings have been given, scores will be combined. Different parts of the examination usually have different weights. For example, the written test might count 60 percent of the final grade, and a rating of training and experience 40 percent. In many jurisdictions, veterans will have a certain number of points added to their grades.

After the final grade has been determined, the names are placed in grade order and an eligible list is established. There are various methods for resolving ties between those who get the same final grade – probably the most common is to place first the name of the person whose application was received first. Job offers are made from the eligible list in the order the names appear on it. You will be notified of your grade and your rank as soon as all these computations have been made. This will be done as rapidly as possible.

People who are found to meet the requirements in the announcement are called "eligibles." Their names are put on a list of eligible candidates. An eligible's chances of getting a job depend on how high he stands on this list and how fast agencies are filling jobs from the list.

When a job is to be filled from a list of eligibles, the agency asks for the names of people on the list of eligibles for that job. When the civil service commission receives this request, it sends to the agency the names of the three people highest on this list. Or, if the job to be filled has specialized requirements, the office sends the agency the names of the top three persons who meet these requirements from the general list.

The appointing officer makes a choice from among the three people whose names were sent to him. If the selected person accepts the appointment, the names of the others are put back on the list to be considered for future openings.

That is the rule in hiring from all kinds of eligible lists, whether they are for typist, carpenter, chemist, or something else. For every vacancy, the appointing officer has his choice of any one of the top three eligibles on the list. This explains why the person whose name is on top of the list sometimes does not get an appointment when some of the persons lower on the list do. If the appointing officer chooses the second or third eligible, the No. 1 eligible does not get a job at once, but stays on the list until he is appointed or the list is terminated.

X. HOW TO PASS THE INTERVIEW TEST

The examination for which you applied requires an oral interview test. You have already taken the written test and you are now being called for the interview test – the final part of the formal examination.

You may think that it is not possible to prepare for an interview test and that there are no procedures to follow during an interview. Our purpose is to point out some things you can do in advance that will help you and some good rules to follow and pitfalls to avoid while you are being interviewed.

What is an interview supposed to test?

The written examination is designed to test the technical knowledge and competence of the candidate; the oral is designed to evaluate intangible qualities, not readily measured otherwise, and to establish a list showing the relative fitness of each candidate – as measured against his competitors – for the position sought. Scoring is not on the basis of "right" and "wrong," but on a sliding scale of values ranging from "not passable" to "outstanding." As a matter of fact, it is possible to achieve a relatively low score without a single "incorrect" answer because of evident weakness in the qualities being measured.

Occasionally, an examination may consist entirely of an oral test – either an individual or a group oral. In such cases, information is sought concerning the technical knowledges and abilities of the candidate, since there has been no written examination for this purpose. More commonly, however, an oral test is used to supplement a written examination.

Who conducts interviews?

The composition of oral boards varies among different jurisdictions. In nearly all, a representative of the personnel department serves as chairman. One of the members of the board may be a representative of the department in which the candidate would work. In some cases, "outside experts" are used, and, frequently, a businessman or some other representative of the general public is asked to serve. Labor and management or other special groups may be represented. The aim is to secure the services of experts in the appropriate field.

However the board is composed, it is a good idea (and not at all improper or unethical) to ascertain in advance of the interview who the members are and what groups they represent. When you are introduced to them, you will have some idea of their backgrounds and interests, and at least you will not stutter and stammer over their names.

What should be done before the interview?

While knowledge about the board members is useful and takes some of the surprise element out of the interview, there is other preparation which is more substantive. It *is* possible to prepare for an oral interview – in several ways:

1) Keep a copy of your application and review it carefully before the interview

This may be the only document before the oral board, and the starting point of the interview. Know what education and experience you have listed there, and the sequence and dates of all of it. Sometimes the board will ask you to review the highlights of your experience for them; you should not have to hem and haw doing it.

2) Study the class specification and the examination announcement

Usually, the oral board has one or both of these to guide them. The qualities, characteristics or knowledges required by the position sought are stated in these documents. They offer valuable clues as to the nature of the oral interview. For example, if the job involves supervisory responsibilities, the announcement will usually indicate that knowledge of modern supervisory methods and the qualifications of the candidate as a supervisor will be tested. If so, you can expect such questions, frequently in the form of a hypothetical situation which you are expected to solve. NEVER go into an oral without knowledge of the duties and responsibilities of the job you seek.

3) Think through each qualification required

Try to visualize the kind of questions you would ask if you were a board member. How well could you answer them? Try especially to appraise your own knowledge and background in each area, *measured against the job sought*, and identify any areas in which you are weak. Be critical and realistic – do not flatter yourself.

4) Do some general reading in areas in which you feel you may be weak

For example, if the job involves supervision and your past experience has NOT, some general reading in supervisory methods and practices, particularly in the field of human relations, might be useful. Do NOT study agency procedures or detailed manuals. The oral board will be testing your understanding and capacity, not your memory.

5) Get a good night's sleep and watch your general health and mental attitude

You will want a clear head at the interview. Take care of a cold or any other minor ailment, and of course, no hangovers.

What should be done on the day of the interview?

Now comes the day of the interview itself. Give yourself plenty of time to get there. Plan to arrive somewhat ahead of the scheduled time, particularly if your appointment is in the fore part of the day. If a previous candidate fails to appear, the board might be ready for you a bit early. By early afternoon an oral board is almost invariably behind schedule if there are many candidates, and you may have to wait. Take along a book or magazine to read, or your application to review, but leave any extraneous material in the waiting room when you go in for your interview. In any event, relax and compose yourself.

The matter of dress is important. The board is forming impressions about you – from your experience, your manners, your attitude, and your appearance. Give your personal appearance careful attention. Dress your best, but not your flashiest. Choose conservative, appropriate clothing, and be sure it is immaculate. This is a business interview, and your appearance should indicate that you regard it as such. Besides, being well groomed and properly dressed will help boost your confidence.

Sooner or later, someone will call your name and escort you into the interview room. *This is it.* From here on you are on your own. It is too late for any more preparation. But remember, you asked for this opportunity to prove your fitness, and you are here because your request was granted.

What happens when you go in?

The usual sequence of events will be as follows: The clerk (who is often the board stenographer) will introduce you to the chairman of the oral board, who will introduce you to the other members of the board. Acknowledge the introductions before you sit down. Do not be surprised if you find a microphone facing you or a stenotypist sitting by. Oral interviews are usually recorded in the event of an appeal or other review.

Usually the chairman of the board will open the interview by reviewing the highlights of your education and work experience from your application – primarily for the benefit of the other members of the board, as well as to get the material into the record. Do not interrupt or comment unless there is an error or significant misinterpretation; if that is the case, do not hesitate. But do not quibble about insignificant matters. Also, he will usually ask you some question about your education, experience or your present job – partly to get you to start talking and to establish the interviewing "rapport." He may start the actual questioning, or turn it over to one of the other members. Frequently, each member undertakes the questioning on a particular area, one in which he is perhaps most competent, so you can expect each member to participate in the examination. Because time is limited, you may also expect some rather abrupt switches in the direction the questioning takes, so do not be upset by it. Normally, a board member will not pursue a single line of questioning unless he discovers a particular strength or weakness.

After each member has participated, the chairman will usually ask whether any member has any further questions, then will ask you if you have anything you wish to add. Unless you are expecting this question, it may floor you. Worse, it may start you off on an extended, extemporaneous speech. The board is not usually seeking more information. The question is principally to offer you a last opportunity to present further qualifications or to indicate that you have nothing to add. So, if you feel that a significant qualification or characteristic has been overlooked, it is proper to point it out in a sentence or so. Do not compliment the board on the thoroughness of their examination – they have been sketchy, and you know it. If you wish, merely say, "No thank you, I have nothing further to add." This is a point where you can "talk yourself out" of a good impression or fail to present an important bit of information. Remember, *you close the interview yourself.*

The chairman will then say, "That is all, Mr. _____, thank you." Do not be startled; the interview is over, and quicker than you think. Thank him, gather your belongings and take your leave. Save your sigh of relief for the other side of the door.

How to put your best foot forward

Throughout this entire process, you may feel that the board individually and collectively is trying to pierce your defenses, seek out your hidden weaknesses and embarrass and confuse you. Actually, this is not true. They are obliged to make an appraisal of your qualifications for the job you are seeking, and they want to see you in your best light. Remember, they must interview all candidates and a non-cooperative candidate may become a failure in spite of their best efforts to bring out his qualifications. Here are 15 suggestions that will help you:

1) **Be natural – Keep your attitude confident, not cocky**

If you are not confident that you can do the job, do not expect the board to be. Do not apologize for your weaknesses, try to bring out your strong points. The board is interested in a positive, not negative, presentation. Cockiness will antagonize any board member and make him wonder if you are covering up a weakness by a false show of strength.

2) **Get comfortable, but don't lounge or sprawl**

Sit erectly but not stiffly. A careless posture may lead the board to conclude that you are careless in other things, or at least that you are not impressed by the importance of the occasion. Either conclusion is natural, even if incorrect. Do not fuss with your clothing, a pencil or an ashtray. Your hands may occasionally be useful to emphasize a point; do not let them become a point of distraction.

3) **Do not wisecrack or make small talk**

This is a serious situation, and your attitude should show that you consider it as such. Further, the time of the board is limited – they do not want to waste it, and neither should you.

4) Do not exaggerate your experience or abilities

In the first place, from information in the application or other interviews and sources, the board may know more about you than you think. Secondly, you probably will not get away with it. An experienced board is rather adept at spotting such a situation, so do not take the chance.

5) If you know a board member, do not make a point of it, yet do not hide it

Certainly you are not fooling him, and probably not the other members of the board. Do not try to take advantage of your acquaintanceship – it will probably do you little good.

6) Do not dominate the interview

Let the board do that. They will give you the clues – do not assume that you have to do all the talking. Realize that the board has a number of questions to ask you, and do not try to take up all the interview time by showing off your extensive knowledge of the answer to the first one.

7) Be attentive

You only have 20 minutes or so, and you should keep your attention at its sharpest throughout. When a member is addressing a problem or question to you, give him your undivided attention. Address your reply principally to him, but do not exclude the other board members.

8) Do not interrupt

A board member may be stating a problem for you to analyze. He will ask you a question when the time comes. Let him state the problem, and wait for the question.

9) Make sure you understand the question

Do not try to answer until you are sure what the question is. If it is not clear, restate it in your own words or ask the board member to clarify it for you. However, do not haggle about minor elements.

10) Reply promptly but not hastily

A common entry on oral board rating sheets is "candidate responded readily," or "candidate hesitated in replies." Respond as promptly and quickly as you can, but do not jump to a hasty, ill-considered answer.

11) Do not be peremptory in your answers

A brief answer is proper – but do not fire your answer back. That is a losing game from your point of view. The board member can probably ask questions much faster than you can answer them.

12) Do not try to create the answer you think the board member wants

He is interested in what kind of mind you have and how it works – not in playing games. Furthermore, he can usually spot this practice and will actually grade you down on it.

13) Do not switch sides in your reply merely to agree with a board member

Frequently, a member will take a contrary position merely to draw you out and to see if you are willing and able to defend your point of view. Do not start a debate, yet do not surrender a good position. If a position is worth taking, it is worth defending.

14) Do not be afraid to admit an error in judgment if you are shown to be wrong

The board knows that you are forced to reply without any opportunity for careful consideration. Your answer may be demonstrably wrong. If so, admit it and get on with the interview.

15) Do not dwell at length on your present job

The opening question may relate to your present assignment. Answer the question but do not go into an extended discussion. You are being examined for a *new* job, not your present one. As a matter of fact, try to phrase ALL your answers in terms of the job for which you are being examined.

Basis of Rating

Probably you will forget most of these "do's" and "don'ts" when you walk into the oral interview room. Even remembering them all will not ensure you a passing grade. Perhaps you did not have the qualifications in the first place. But remembering them will help you to put your best foot forward, without treading on the toes of the board members.

Rumor and popular opinion to the contrary notwithstanding, an oral board wants you to make the best appearance possible. They know you are under pressure – but they also want to see how you respond to it as a guide to what your reaction would be under the pressures of the job you seek. They will be influenced by the degree of poise you display, the personal traits you show and the manner in which you respond.

ABOUT THIS BOOK

This book contains tests divided into Examination Sections. Go through each test, answering every question in the margin. We have also attached a sample answer sheet at the back of the book that can be removed and used. At the end of each test look at the answer key and check your answers. On the ones you got wrong, look at the right answer choice and learn. Do not fill in the answers first. Do not memorize the questions and answers, but understand the answer and principles involved. On your test, the questions will likely be different from the samples. Questions are changed and new ones added. If you understand these past questions you should have success with any changes that arise. Tests may consist of several types of questions. We have additional books on each subject should more study be advisable or necessary for you. Finally, the more you study, the better prepared you will be. This book is intended to be the last thing you study before you walk into the examination room. Prior study of relevant texts is also recommended. NLC publishes some of these in our Fundamental Series. Knowledge and good sense are important factors in passing your exam. Good luck also helps. So now study this Passbook, absorb the material contained within and take that knowledge into the examination. Then do your best to pass that exam.

EXAMINATION SECTION

EXAMINATION SECTION
TEST 1

DIRECTIONS: Each question or incomplete statement is followed by several suggested answers or completions. Select the one that BEST answers the question or completes the statement. *PRINT THE LETTER OF THE CORRECT ANSWER IN THE SPACE AT THE RIGHT.*

1. When filling an empty aqueduct, the valve should be opened

    A. slowly to prevent damage to the aqueduct
    B. rapidly to fill the line as soon as possible
    C. slowly to prevent rapid lowering of the reservoir level
    D. rapidly so that there are no air locks

2. The BEST way of detecting the location of a suspected chlorine leak is by placing a _____ near the suspected leak.

    A. rag, which has been dipped in a strong ammonia water,
    B. match
    C. piece of litmus paper
    D. flow meter

3. The term *run-off* refers to the

    A. amount a valve must be turned in order to open it fully
    B. length of time an electric motor continues to turn after the current is shut off
    C. amount of rainfall which flows from the ground surface into the streams and reservoirs
    D. distance the water falls from the intake gate to the turbine

4. Algae in reservoirs may be killed by using

    A. zeolite   B. copper sulphate
    C. sodium chloride   D. calcium chloride

5. The one of the following types of valves that USUALLY operates without manual control is a(n) _____ valve.

    A. check   B. globe   C. gate   D. angle

6. Rate of flow of water through a water treatment plant is USUALLY referred to in terms of

    A. c.f.s.   B. c.f.m.   C. r.p.m.   D. m.g.d.

7. In order to make it easier to operate a large valve or gate, pressures on both sides of the valve or gate are balanced by

    A. using weights on each side of the valve or gate
    B. opening a smaller by-pass valve
    C. partially shutting down the water in the upstream line
    D. opening the downstream valve very slowly

8. Leaves are removed from the water entering the treatment plant or aqueduct by

    A. skimming   B. coagulating   C. draining   D. screening

9. Odors, due to gases in the water, are removed by

   A. surging   B. sluicing   C. aerating   D. clarifying

10. Chlorine residual refers to the

    A. amount of chlorine that must be added to the water
    B. amount of chlorine that remains in the water after a given period
    C. method of adding the chlorine to the water
    D. method of protecting personnel using chlorine from the effects of the chlorine

11. One of the processes that takes place in an Imhoff tank is

    A. oxidation   B. flocculation   C. digestion   D. coagulation

12. As used in a sewage disposal plant, *effluent* refers to the

    A. basic treatment process of sewage
    B. time it takes for complete treatment of sewage
    C. type of control the plant uses for treatment
    D. final liquid coming out of the treatment process

13. A grit chamber operates on the basis that

    A. grit will settle out of slow-moving water
    B. grit will float and can be removed by skimming the surface
    C. increasing the rate of flow of water will leave the grit behind
    D. spraying water into the air will cause the heavier grit to separate from the water

14. The purpose of sedimentation in any sewage treatment process is to

    A. aerate the sewage
    B. increase the chlorine content of the sewage
    C. remove suspended matter from the sewage
    D. kill the bacteria in the sewage

15. The final treatment for sludge before it is disposed of is

    A. drying   B. adding chlorine
    C. mixing   D. washing

16. The amount of sewage applied to a filter bed is GENERALLY controlled by a

    A. sluice gate   B. flow meter
    C. dosing siphon   D. regulating valve

17. Methane gas which results from the sewage treatment process is MOST frequently

    A. vented to the outside air to prevent injury to plant personnel
    B. used as a fuel in the plant
    C. combined with other gases to render it harmless
    D. burned in the open air

18. The filtering material in a *filter bed* at a sewage treat- ment plant is USUALLY

    A. activated charcoal   B. sand
    C. alum   D. ammonium chloride

19. Cleaning sewer lines is USUALLY done by the use of a   19.____

    A. catch basin   B. flushometer
    C. sewer rod   D. center line

20. One of the ways of locating a leak in a water line is by using a   20.____

    A. manometer   B. sounding rod
    C. poling board   D. diffusor

21. MOST sewer pipes are made of   21.____

    A. cast iron   B. agricultural tile
    C. brass   D. copper

22. One of the materials generally used in caulking joints in bell and spigot pipe is   22.____

    A. tar   B. litharge   C. red lead   D. oakum

23. Water pipe must be laid at least two feet below the ground surface MAINLY to   23.____

    A. prevent freezing
    B. discourage malicious tampering
    C. reduce the pressure required to make the water flow
    D. eliminate possibility of damage to roads in case of water main break

24. When soldering copper gutters, the flux that is GENERALLY used is   24.____

    A. sal ammoniac   B. resin
    C. killed muriatic acid   D. calcium chloride

25. A good concrete mix for use in the foundations of a small building is   25.____

    A. 1:2:5   B. 5:2:1   C. 2:5:1   D. 1:5:2

26. When painting steel, red lead is used MAINLY as a   26.____

    A. primer coat so final coat will adhere better
    B. primer coat to protect the steel from rusting
    C. finish coat to protect the steel from the action of the sun and water
    D. second coat to bind the primer and finish coats

27. Studs in frame buildings are USUALLY   27.____

    A. 1" x 4"   B. 1" x 6"   C. 2" x 4"   D. 2" x 6"

28. A cement mortar used in brickwork is USUALLY made more workable by adding   28.____

    A. phosphate   B. lime   C. calcium   D. grout

Questions 29-32.

DIRECTIONS: The following four questions numbered 29 to 32, inclusive, are to be answered in accordance with the rules of the department of water supply, gas and electricity.

29. The term *water course* refers to

    A. aqueducts only
    B. pipe lines only
    C. natural or artificial streams only
    D. all of the above

30. Where a swimming pool discharges upon or into the ground and the water is not treated, the minimum distance between such discharge and a stream MUST be at least _____ feet.

    A. 50   B. 100   C. 250   D. 450

31. According to the above rules, clothes may

    A. be washed in a spring, if the spring does not feed directly into a reservoir
    B. be washed in a spring if the place where this is being done is at least one mile from a reservoir
    C. be washed in a spring provided a chlorinated soap is used
    D. not be washed in a spring

32. Industrial wastes may

    A. be discharged into a stream provided the stream does not feed directly into a reservoir
    B. be discharged into a stream, provided the point of discharge is at least one mile from a reservoir
    C. be discharged into a stream if the wastes are purified in an approved manner
    D. not be discharged into a stream

33. One method of determining the height of the water in a stream feeding into a reservoir is by means of a

    A. venturi meter   B. flow meter
    C. hook gage   D. strain gage

34. When digging a deep trench, the sides are USUALLY prevented from caving in by using

    A. shoulders   B. blocking   C. pins   D. sheathing

35. The FIRST precaution a worker should take before entering a sewer manhole is to

    A. put on hard-toed shoes
    B. put on safety goggles
    C. check that the next manhole upstream is not obstructed
    D. test the air in the manhole

36. Assume that a fuse blows upon connecting a light load to the circuit. You replace it with the same size fuse, and again the fuse blows.
    The BEST thing to do in this case is to

    A. connect a wire across the fuse so it cannot blow under such a light load
    B. replace the fuse with one having a higher rating
    C. check the wiring of the circuit
    D. place two fuses in series to prevent blowing

37. Of the following material, the one that is BEST for fill as a subgrade for a road is   37.____

    A. sand
    B. silt
    C. clay
    D. a mixture of sand, silt, and clay

38. When dealing with leaking chlorine, it is IMPORTANT to remember that chlorine is   38.____

    A. highly flammable
    B. made safe by spraying water on it
    C. not corrosive
    D. heavier than air

39. Cast iron pipe is MOST frequently cut with a(n)   39.____

    A. hack saw
    B. diamond point chisel
    C. burning torch
    D. abrasive wheel

40. Water hammer in a pipe line is BEST reduced by installing   40.____

    A. a pressure regulator
    B. an air chamber
    C. smaller pipes and valves
    D. larger pipes and valves

KEY (CORRECT ANSWERS)

1. A	11. C	21. A	31. D
2. A	12. D	22. D	32. D
3. C	13. A	23. A	33. C
4. B	14. C	24. C	34. D
5. A	15. A	25. A	35. D
6. D	16. C	26. B	36. C
7. B	17. B	27. C	37. D
8. D	18. B	28. B	38. D
9. C	19. C	29. D	39. B
10. B	20. B	30. B	40. B

TEST 2

DIRECTIONS: Each question or incomplete statement is followed by several suggested answers or completions. Select the one that BEST answers the question or completes the statement. *PRINT THE LETTER OF THE CORRECT ANSWER IN SPACE AT THE RIGHT.*

1. When used in conjunction with a centrifugal pump, a foot valve   1.____

    A. equalizes the pressure on both sides of the pump
    B. regulates the amount of water flowing through the pump
    C. prevents water in the pump from flowing back down the suction line
    D. adjusts the speed of the pump to the amount of water to be pumped

2. Grounding an electric motor is   2.____

    A. *good* practice because the motor will operate better
    B. *poor* practice because the motor will not operate as well
    C. *good* practice because it protects against shock hazards
    D. *poor* practice because it increases shock hazards

3. The one of the following wrenches that should NOT be used to turn a nut is a ___ wrench.   3.____

    A. monkey   B. box   C. stillson   D. socket

4. A drill is GENERALLY removed from the chuck of a portable electric drill by using a   4.____

    A. drift pin   B. wedge
    C. centerpunch   D. key

5. The finished surface of a dirt road is MOST frequently maintained with a   5.____

    A. blade grader   B. bulldozer
    C. dragline   D. carryall

6. Frequent stalling of a truck engine is MOST probably due to a   6.____

    A. weak battery   B. low battery water level
    C. leaking oil filter   D. dirty carburetor

7. If the reading of the oil pressure gage on a gasoline motor should suddenly drop to zero, the FIRST thing the operator should do is to   7.____

    A. check the filter
    B. inspect the oil lines
    C. tighten the oil pan bolts
    D. stop the motor

8. A tractor is to be stored for two months. In order to keep it in BEST condition, it should be   8.____

    A. drained of all fuel and oil
    B. lubricated every week
    C. started up periodically and run until warm
    D. steam cleaned and all water drained from the radiator

9. Trees suffering from transplanting shock are quickly helped by   9.____

A. deep watering		B. foliage feeding	
C. root feeding		D. vitamin treatments	

10. For MOST rapid healing, trees should be pruned during

    A. November, December, and January
    B. February, March, and April
    C. May, June, and July
    D. August, September, and October

11. The blades of a lawn mower should be set so that the blades

    A. firmly touch the bed knife
    B. barely touch the bed knife
    C. clear the bed knife by 1/16 inch
    D. clear the bed knife by 1/8 inch

12. The MAIN reason for mulching is to

    A. fertilize the soil
    B. prevent erosion
    C. protect plants from the cold
    D. kill insects

13. A compost heap would MOST likely include

    A. lawn clippings   B. sand
    C. stumps of trees   D. gravel

14. Of the following statements with regard to *seeding,* the one that is CORRECT is:

    A. Seeds should be sown on a windy day
    B. The ground should be watered heavily after seeding
    C. Seeding should be done primarily on a bright and sunny day
    D. It is not necessary to carefully apportion the amount of seeds sown

15. Organic matter is often added to soil to better condition it for growing plants.
    Of the following, the item that is NOT organic matter is

    A. lime   B. peat   C. manure   D. leaf mold

16. Of the following, the BEST way to store coniferous seedlings which cannot be planted for a few days is to

    A. unwrap them and put them in a dark, dry location
    B. place them flat on the ground in a sunny location so they can get plenty of light and air
    C. place them in a trench dug in the earth and cover the root ends with soil
    D. make sure the ball is not loosened and keep in a hothouse

17. Transplanting of seedlings is BEST done in early

    A. spring   B. summer   C. autumn   D. winter

18. After planting privet hedges, they are frequently cut back to within a few inches of the ground.
    This is USUALLY done to

    A. remove dead parts of the hedge
    B. insure dense growth from the ground up
    C. speed up root development
    D. reduce the possibility of insect damage while the hedge is taking root

18.____

19. *Heaving* of pavements in wintertime is USUALLY caused by the

    A. difference of expansion of pavement and subgrade
    B. freezing of water in subgrade
    C. loss of bond between pavement and subgrade
    D. brittleness of pavement

19.____

20. Erosion of side slopes caused by the action of water is GREATEST when the soil is

    A. silt   B. clay   C. hardpan   D. silty-clay

20.____

21. The MAIN reason for making a crown in a road pavement is to

    A. reduce the amount of paving material necessary
    B. make it easier for cars to go around a curve
    C. drain surface water
    D. increase the strength of the pavement where it is most needed

21.____

22. The MAIN reason for paving ditches at the side of a road is to

    A. prevent damage from cars
    B. permit the ditch to carry more water
    C. prevent erosion of the soil in the ditch
    D. block water from getting under the pavement

22.____

23. Assume that vitrified clay tile pipe, with open joints, is being used as the underdrain for a roadway.
    This pipe should be laid

    A. directly on the bottom of the trench
    B. on a bed of clay
    C. on a bed of peat
    D. on a bed of gravel

23.____

24. A macadam road is one in which the base is GENERALLY made of

    A. asphalt   B. broken stone
    C. concrete   D. stabilized soil

24.____

25. To loosen compacted rocky earth road surfaces, the BEST piece of equipment to use is a

    A. disc harrow   B. drag line   C. bulldozer   D. scarifier

25.____

26. Oiling of an earth road is BEST done

    A. in the winter before the snow falls
    B. when you expect much rain

26.____

C. in the spring during dry weather
D. immediately after snow is cleared from the road

27. Cracks in concrete roads are BEST repaired by filling them with 27.____

    A. tar   B. grout
    C. mineral filler   D. sand

28. When repairing patches in old asphalt pavements, the edges of the patch should FIRST 28.____
    be painted with

    A. the same material used for the patch
    B. kerosene
    C. asphalt cement
    D. asphalt binder

29. The sum of 3 1/4, 5 1/8, 2 1/2, and 3 3/8 is 29.____

    A. 14   B. 14 1/8   C. 14 1/4   D. 14 3/8

30. Assume that it takes 6 men 8 days to do a particular job. 30.____
    If you have only 4 men available to do this job and they all work at the same speed,
    then the number of days it would take to complete the job would be

    A. 11   B. 12   C. 13   D. 14

31. The city aims to supply *potable* water. As used in this sentence, the word *potable* means 31.____
    MOST NEARLY

    A. clear   B. drinkable   C. fresh   D. adequate

32. Water, after being purified, should not be turbid. As used in this sentence, the word turbid 32.____
    means MOST NEARLY

    A. cloudy   B. warm   C. infected D. hard

33. The flow of water is *impeded* by the silt in the bottom of the stream. 33.____
    As used in this sentence, the word *impeded* means MOST NEARLY

    A. dammed   B. hindered   C. helped   D. dirtied

Questions 34-35.

DIRECTIONS: Questions 34 and 35 are based on the following paragraph.

Repeated burning of the same area should be avoided. Burning should not be done on impervious, shallow, unstable, or highly erodible soils, or on steep slopes - especially in areas subject to heavy rains or rapid snowmelt. When existing vegetation is likely to be killed or seriously weakened by the fire, measures should be taken to assure prompt revegetation of the burned area. Burns should be limited to relatively small proportions of a watershed unit so that the stream channels will be able to carry any increased flows with a minimum of damage.

34. According to the above paragraph, planned burning should be limited to small areas of the watershed because 34.____

   A. the fire can be better controlled
   B. existing vegetation will be less likely to be killed
   C. plants will grow quicker in small areas
   D. there will be less likelihood of damaging floods

35. According to the above paragraph, burning usually should be done on soils that 35.____

   A. readily absorb moisture
   B. have been burnt before
   C. exist as a thin layer over rock
   D. can be flooded by nearby streams

36. If a foreman does not understand the instructions that are given to him by the district engineer, the BEST thing to do is to 36.____

   A. work out the solution to the problem himself
   B. do the job in the way he thinks is best
   C. get one of the other foremen to do the job
   D. ask that the instructions be repeated and clarified

37. The BEST foreman is the one who 37.____

   A. can work as fast as the fastest man in the crew
   B. is the most skilled mechanic
   C. can get the most work out of the men
   D. is the strongest man

38. Complimenting a man for good work is 38.____

   A. *good* practice since it will give the man an incentive to continue working well
   B. *poor* practice because the other men will become jealous
   C. *good* practice because in the future the foreman will not have to supervise this man
   D. *poor* practice since the man should work well without needing compliments

39. In dealing with his men, it is MOST important that a foreman be 39.____

   A. a disciplinarian   B. stern
   C. fair   D. chummy with his men

40. When issuing a violation to a member of the public, it is MOST important that a foreman be 40.____

   A. aloof and refuse to discuss the violation
   B. stern, and warn the person to correct the violation immediately
   C. courteous and explain what must be done to correct the violation
   D. friendly and volunteer assistance to correct the violation

KEY (CORRECT ANSWERS)

1.	C	11.	B	21.	C	31.	B
2.	C	12.	C	22.	C	32.	A
3.	C	13.	A	23.	D	33.	B
4.	D	14.	B	24.	B	34.	D
5.	A	15.	A	25.	D	35.	A
6.	D	16.	C	26.	C	36.	D
7.	D	17.	A	27.	A	37.	C
8.	C	18.	B	28.	C	38.	A
9.	B	19.	B	29.	C	39.	C
10.	B	20.	A	30.	B	40.	C

EXAMINATION SECTION
TEST 1

DIRECTIONS: Each question or incomplete statement is followed by several suggested answers or completions. Select the one that BEST answers the question or completes the statement. *PRINT THE LETTER OF THE CORRECT ANSWER IN THE SPACE AT THE RIGHT.*

1. When changes, which the men might not like, are made in construction methods, a GOOD Foreman should

    A. tell the men to adopt the new methods and not to bother him with questions
    B. assign a senior man in his crew to instruct the men in the new methods and tell the senior man that he has full responsibility for the instructions
    C. explain to the men that he does not like the new methods, but that it was not his decision to make
    D. explain to the men, as far as possible, all the reasons for adopting the new methods

2. When a citizen complains, to a Foreman that the equipment on a job under his supervision is causing too much noise, the Foreman should

    A. tell the citizen that the project will soon be finished
    B. investigate the complaint to see if it is valid
    C. stop all work immediately
    D. ignore the complaint

3. Participation of foremen in employee safety training programs as instructors should be

    A. encouraged since it is a means of enhancing motivation
    B. discouraged since it is poor policy to let the men see the foremen work
    C. discouraged since it wastes the foremen's time
    D. required since the foremen are the only ones qualified to instruct

4. When training a group of trainees, the Foreman should

    A. set up a rigid program assuming that all trainees have the same skills
    B. eliminate any trainee who does not demonstrate aptitude in all types of work
    C. adjust the program to account for individual differences in trainees
    D. eliminate any topics which the trainees do not want

5. If a new man in a Foreman's crew feels that he cannot perform a specific task, the Foreman should

    A. transfer the new man to another crew
    B. give the new man the necessary training to do it
    C. tell the new man he has to learn on his own time to do the task
    D. tell the new man he is expected to do the task as best as he can

6. The encouragement by a Foreman of competition between trainees in a training program is

    A. *inadvisable* because some trainees perform better than others
    B. *advisable* because it provides an incentive to the trainees

C. *inadvisable* because they are all paid at the same rate
D. *advisable* because the Foreman will have more free time

7. It is necessary to shut off the water in a main temporarily in order to make repairs. In order to get cooperation from the general public, the

   A. job should be done at night so that few people will be aware of it
   B. shut-off crew should be ordered not to speak to the general public
   C. job should be done in several stages so that the public realizes how difficult the problem is
   D. purpose and duration of the shut-off should be explained to the general public

8. Of the following, the one which a Foreman should NOT do if he wants the willing cooperation of his men is

   A. do everything in his power to provide his men with adequate equipment
   B. praise his men after they do an exceptional job
   C. use authority sparingly
   D. show favoritism to the men who do not complain about the work

9. When a new employee joins a Foreman's crew, the Foreman should

   A. guide the new employee through the adjustment period in a friendly, sympathetic manner
   B. speak to the new employee as little as possible
   C. avoid the new employee completely
   D. give the new employee no responsibility

10. When a man with many years of service is transferred to a Foreman's crew to perform a type of work at which he is inexperienced, the Foreman should

    A. expect him to know the safety procedures for the new working conditions
    B. not embarrass the man by giving him safety instructions
    C. give him the same safety instructions a new employee gets
    D. assign him to work with the crew that had the latest accident to learn the safety procedures

11. Of the following, the one that is the BEST objective of an employee suggestion program is to

    A. create more jobs
    B. increase work load of each employee
    C. increase idle time between jobs
    D. stimulate employees' interest in their jobs

12. Of the following, the one that is NOT required in order to be an effective Foreman is the ability to

    A. delegate all responsibilities
    B. use proper instructional methods
    C. build morale
    D. discipline wisely

13. Of the following, the FIRST step to be taken by a Foreman when he must make a decision in regard to a construction problem is to

    A. get all the facts
    B. decide
    C. evaluate the facts
    D. make a tentative decision

14. When an employee, who previously had a record of promptness, is frequently late, the BEST action for the Foreman to take in order to correct the employee's lateness is to

    A. ignore the lateness because the employee will come in on time as soon as it is possible to do so
    B. recommend that he be discharged
    C. scold him in front of the rest of the men to set an example
    D. tell him that disciplinary action will be taken if he continues to be late

15. Of the following actions, the one that most probably is NOT an indication that a subordinate has a potential grievance is that the subordinate

    A. very often becomes grouchy and irritable on the job
    B. goes to the washroom more often than usual to read a newspaper
    C. frequently comes to the Foreman with minor suggestions
    D. is frequently late

16. In dealing with grievances, a Foreman should

    A. do whatever is necessary to satisfy the employee
    B. realize that some persons make demands that cannot be met
    C. state the rules and regulations and not discuss the situation further
    D. wait until the situation changes before acting on the grievance

17. If a Foreman detects low morale in his crew, he should FIRST

    A. investigate the causes and attempt to eliminate them
    B. tell top management so that they can find out what is wrong
    C. ignore it
    D. request that at least one-half of the crew be transferred

18. Of the following, the one that is NOT a proper procedure to follow in settling grievances is

    A. settle grievances promptly
    B. settle grievances on merit only
    C. only top management should settle grievances
    D. settle grievances on the basis of as many relevant facts as possible

19. A Foreman is approached by a homeowner who asks the Foreman to have his crew remove a large tree from his backyard and offers the Foreman $25 for doing the work. Of the following, the BEST action for the Foreman to take is to

    A. order his crew to do the work and keep the money
    B. order the crew to do the work and divide the money between his crew
    C. politely refuse to do the work
    D. order his men to do the work and refuse to take any money

20. Of the following, the MOST important purpose of a good report made by a Foreman is to

    A. provide the information needed at the time and on the subject under consideration
    B. justify the manpower expenditure in making the report
    C. eliminate the necessity of each of his subordinates making a report
    D. prevent the public from blaming the department for its action

21. When the men under his supervision are not producing work of the desired quality, the Foreman should FIRST

    A. scold them
    B. find out what is causing the defects
    C. make sure that the men have a good reason for producing poor quality work
    D. notify the District Foreman

22. Under the normal daily working conditions, if Foreman X requests Foreman Y for the services of a laborer, Foreman Y should

    A. send his most capable laborer
    B. send his least capable laborer
    C. ignore Foreman X
    D. refer Foreman X to the District Foreman

23. One of the steps a Foreman should take in order to encourage subordinates to cooperate with him is to

    A. see that tools and materials are available in the right quantity when needed
    B. let his men participate in deciding all important decisions by taking a vote
    C. let his men leave work early at least once a week
    D. try to give them deadlines that are very difficult to meet

24. Sixty-two fittings, each weighing 288 pounds, are used on a job.
    If one ton equals 2,000 pounds, the total weight of the sixty-two fittings is MOST NEARLY _____ tons.

    A. 7.5   B. 7.9   C. 8.3   D. 8.7

25. Five and one-quarter percent of $8,752.00 is

    A. $457.35   B. $458.26   C. $459.48   D. $460.50

26. A slab of concrete is 126 feet long, 36 feet wide, and 9 inches thick.
    Its volume, in cubic yards, is MOST NEARLY

    A. 28   B. 42   C. 126   D. 378

27. A pipe is laid on an upward slope of 1/4" vertical for each one-foot horizontal.
    In a horizontal distance of 30 feet, the vertical distance the pipe rises, in inches, is

    A. 6 7/8   B. 7 1/2   C. 7 7/8   D. 8 1/2

28. A distance of 32 7/8" is MOST NEARLY _____ feet.

    A. 2.54   B. 2.64   C. 2.74   D. 2.84

29. The sum of the numbers 5' 10 7/8", 17' 0 1/2", and 22' 7 1/16" is   29____

    A. 44' 5 5/16"   B. 45' 6 7/16"
    C. 45' 8 1/16"   D. 46' 3 3/16"

30. The difference between 45' 6 1/2" and 27' 8 3/4" is   30____

    A. 18' 4 1/4"   B. 18' 2 3/4"
    C. 17' 11 1/4"   D. 17' 9 3/4"

KEY (CORRECT ANSWERS)

1.	D	16.	B
2.	B	17.	A
3.	A	18.	C
4.	C	19.	C
5.	B	20.	A
6.	B	21.	B
7.	D	22.	D
8.	D	23.	A
9.	A	24.	C
10.	C	25.	C
11.	D	26.	C
12.	A	27.	B
13.	A	28.	C
14.	D	29.	B
15.	C	30.	D

EXAMINATION SECTION
TEST 1

DIRECTIONS: Each question or incomplete statement is followed by several suggested answers or completions. Select the one that BEST answers the question or completes the statement. *PRINT THE LETTER OF THE CORRECT ANSWER IN THE SPACE AT THE RIGHT.*

1. A Bourdon tube gage is used to measure

   A. temperature
   B. acidity
   C. turbidity
   D. pressure

   1.____

2. An instrument used to locate buried metallic pipes is known as a(n)

   A. scleroscope
   B. M-scope
   C. kinoscope
   D. oscilloscope

   2.____

3. The PRIMARY function of a check valve is to

   A. prevent the illegal use of fire hydrants
   B. insure adequate water pressure in high buildings
   C. prevent freezing of water
   D. permit flow of water in one direction only

   3.____

4. Of the following, the torque applied by a ratchet wrench would be expressed in units of

   A. horsepower
   B. pounds
   C. pounds per square inch
   D. foot-pounds

   4.____

5. Most lead joints runners are made of

   A. nylon
   B. asbestos
   C. leadite
   D. polyethylene

   5.____

6. The tool shown in the sketch at the right is a
   A. pickout iron
   B. pipe jointer
   C. cover bolt wrench
   D. pipe reamer

   6.____

7. In order to reduce the force necessary to open or close large gate valves, the valves are equipped with a

   A. vacuum breaker
   B. by-pass
   C. saddle
   D. shear gate

   7.____

8. In order to open a ground-key valve, used as a corporation cock to full flow, it is necessary to rotate the handle _____ degrees.

   A. 45   B. 60   C. 75   D. 90

   8.____

9. A foot valve is MOST often used

   A. to relieve excess pressure in a water main
   B. on the suction pipe of a centrifugal pump
   C. at the high point in a pipeline
   D. to drain a pipeline

10. Of the following tools, the one that generally should NOT be used to tighten screwed piping is a _____ wrench.

    A. Stillson
    B. strap
    C. monkey
    D. chain

11. A 6-inch branch may be connected to an 8-inch main without shutting off the flow of water by using a

    A. tapping valve and sleeve
    B. cutting in tee
    C. cutting in valve and sleeve
    D. pipe tong

12. When water flows through a thirty-second bend, the direction of flow changes

    A. 11 1/4°   B. 22 1/2°   C. 45°   D. 90°

13. A main in which water is flowing east is connected to a pipe offset.
    As the water leaves the offset, it will be flowing toward the

    A. north   B. south   C. east   D. west

14. An electrolysis test connection on a water main is used to measure the

    A. salinity of the ground water outside the main
    B. the chlorine residual in the water in the main
    C. stray electric current in the main
    D. temperature of the ground around the main

15. A common method of temporarily lowering the ground water below the level of operations in a trench is by the use of

    A. wellpoints
    B. mud valves
    C. piles
    D. trenching machines

16. The diameter of a #6 steel reinforcing bar is MOST NEARLY

    A. 1"   B. 3/4"   C. 1/2"   D. 1/4"

17. The quick opening or closing of valves or gates, and the sudden starting, stopping, or variation in speed of pumps is FREQUENTLY the cause of

    A. sluggish flow of water
    B. water-borne diseases
    C. water hammer
    D. water hardness

18. Poured lead pipe joints must be calked MAINLY because the hot lead

    A. corrodes some of the cast iron
    B. burns some of the jute
    C. becomes porous on cooling
    D. shrinks on cooling

19. Flexibility between a water main and a service pipe can be obtained by the use of a   19.____

　　A. corporation cock　　　　　　B. gooseneck
　　C. curb stop　　　　　　　　　　D. air-release valve

20. It is necessary to shut off the water in a main temporarily in order to make repairs.   20.____
　　In order to get cooperation from the general public, the

　　A. job should be done at night so that few people will be aware of it
　　B. shut-off crew should be ordered not to speak to the general public
　　C. job should be done in several stages so that the public realizes how difficult the problem is
　　D. purpose and duration of the shut-off should be explained to the general public

Questions 21-25.

DIRECTIONS: Questions 21 through 25 are to be answered on the basis of maps or diagrams used by departments of water resources.

21. On a distribution map, the symbol ———— — ———— refers to a   21.____
　　main whose diameter is

　　A. 6"　　　　B. 8"　　　　C. 10"　　　　D. 12"

22. On a distribution map, the symbol [symbol] refers to a   22.____

　　A. gate valve　　　　　　B. blow-off
　　C. air-cock　　　　　　　D. regulator

23. On a distribution map, the symbol ——+—— refers to a   23.____

　　A. gate valve　　　　　　B. 3-way
　　C. 4-way　　　　　　　　D. reducer

24. On a distribution map, the symbol ↓ refers to a   24.____

　　A. hydrant　　B. air-cock　　C. 3-way　　D. 4-way

25. On a work area diagram, the symbol [hatched rectangle] refers to a(n)   25.____

　　A. office　　　　　　B. truck
　　C. barricade　　　　D. excavation.

KEY (CORRECT ANSWERS)

1. D
2. B
3. D
4. D
5. B

6. D
7. B
8. D
9. B
10. C

11. A
12. A
13. C
14. C
15. A

16. B
17. C
18. D
19. B
20. D

21. B
22. B
23. A
24. C
25. D

TEST 2

DIRECTIONS: Each question or incomplete statement is followed by several suggested answers or completions. Select the one that BEST answers the question or completes the statement. *PRINT THE LETTER OF THE CORRECT ANSWER IN THE SPACE AT THE RIGHT.*

1. According to standard water main specifications, prior to laying any straight pipe or special castings, the inside surfaces shall be mopped or sprayed with a chlorine solution containing not less than 150 _____ of chlorine.   1.____

   A. quarts B. lbs. C. p.p.m. D. tanks

2. When water main repairs are underway on the north side of a two-way street which runs east and west, the location recommended by the Department of Water Resources of a lead heating burner is _____ of the excavation.   2.____

   A. north B. east C. south D. west

3. Of the following statements, the one which is NOT included on the official water supply shut-off notice is   3.____

   A. turn off water-cooled refrigerating and air conditioning units
   B. close main house valve on water pipe supplying premises
   C. drain all water pipes above the basement
   D. open, as a vent, one hot water faucet above the level of the hot water storage tank

4. In order to obtain a Temporary Street Opening Permit, the applicant must be a   4.____

   A. city resident B. city employee
   C. licensed plumber D. professional engineer

5. In accordance with standard water main specifications, all water mains 20 inches in diameter or larger shall be subjected to a leakage test at a pressure of 125 psi.
   The leakage shall NOT be greater than   5.____

   A. twenty gallons per 24 hours
   B. two gallons per linear foot of pipe joint per 24 hours
   C. two gallons per linear foot of pipe joint per 20 minutes
   D. twenty gallons per mile of pipe per 24 hours

6. In accordance with official specifications, in paved streets the length of trench that may be opened between the point where the backfilling has been completed and the point where the pavement is being removed shall NOT exceed   6.____

   A. the width of the street
   B. fifteen hundred feet for pipes 24 inches or less in diameter
   C. five hundred feet for all pipe diameters
   D. the distance between hydrants

Questions 7-10.

DIRECTIONS: Questions 7 through 10 are to be answered SOLELY on the basis of the following passage.

The choice of equipment to be used in excavating a trench will depend on the job conditions, the depth and width of the trench, the class of the soil, the extent to which ground water is present, the width of the right of way for the disposal of excavated earth, and the type of equipment already owned by a contractor.

If a relatively shallow and narrow trench is to be excavated in firm soil, the wheel-type trenching machine is probably the most suitable. However, if the soil is rock, which requires blasting, the most suitable excavator will be a hoe, or a less desirable substitute could be a dragline. If the soil is unstable, water-saturated material, it may be necessary to use a dragline, hoe, or clamshell and let the walls establish a stable slope. If it is necessary to install solid sheeting to hold the walls in place, neither a hoe nor a dragline will work satisfactorily. A clamshell, which can excavate between the trench braces that hold the sheeting in place, probably will be the best equipment for the job.

7. According to the above passage, the wheel-type trenching machine is probably the MOST suitable for excavating

    A. unstable, water-saturated material
    B. when it is necessary to install solid sheeting
    C. a relatively shallow and narrow trench in firm soil
    D. when ground water is present

8. According to the above passage, the width of the right of way for the disposal of excavated earth

    A. depends upon the width of the street
    B. affects the depth of cover
    C. affects the choice of equipment to be used in excavating
    D. should be minimized to avoid inconveniencing the public

9. According to the above passage, a hoe will be the MOST suitable excavator if the

    A. soil is rock which requires blasting
    B. equipment is already owned by a contractor
    C. trench requires solid sheeting
    D. trench is over twenty feet deep

10. According to the above passage, the BEST equipment to use for excavating when it is necessary to install solid sheeting to hold the walls in place probably will be a

    A. clamshell
    B. dragline
    C. hoe
    D. wheel-type trenching machine

Questions 11-12.

DIRECTIONS: Questions 11 and 12 are to be answered SOLELY on the basis of the following passage.

Construction pumps frequently are required to perform under severe conditions, such as resulting from variations in the pumping head or from handling water that is muddy, sandy and trashy, or highly corrosive. The rate of pumping may vary several hundred percent during the period of construction. The most satisfactory solution to the pumping problem may be a single all-purpose pump, or it may be to use several types and sizes of pumps, to permit flexibility in the operations. The proper solution is to select the equipment which will take care of the pumping needs adequately at the lowest total cost.

11. According to the above passage, the PROPER solution to a construction pumping problem is to select equipment that has the lowest total cost which will also

    A. perform under severe conditions
    B. take care of the pumping needs adequately
    C. permit flexibility in operations
    D. provide maximum safety

12. According to the above passage, a variation of several hundred percent during the period of construction may occur in the

    A. pumping head
    B. rate of pumping
    C. volume of sandy and trashy water
    D. volume of highly corrosive water

Questions 13-14.

DIRECTIONS: Questions 13 and 14 are to be answered SOLELY on the basis of the following passage.

The mechanical failure of equipment may be the cause of a serious accident. Competent maintenance of equipment will reduce mechanical failures and in so doing reduce injuries and construction interruptions. Regular inspection of equipment will reduce maintenance expense.

13. Of the following, the BEST title for the above passage is

    A. Construction Productivity
    B. Preventive Maintenance of Equipment
    C. Inspection of Equipment
    D. Economical Construction

14. According to the above passage, the way to save money in construction work is to

    A. have qualified people operate equipment
    B. have periodic inspection of equipment
    C. have regular overhaul of equipment
    D. start a maintenance training program

15. Of the following items, the one MOST suitable for measuring the flow of water in a pipe is a

    A. poppet   B. hydraulic ram
    C. cistern   D. pitometer

16.

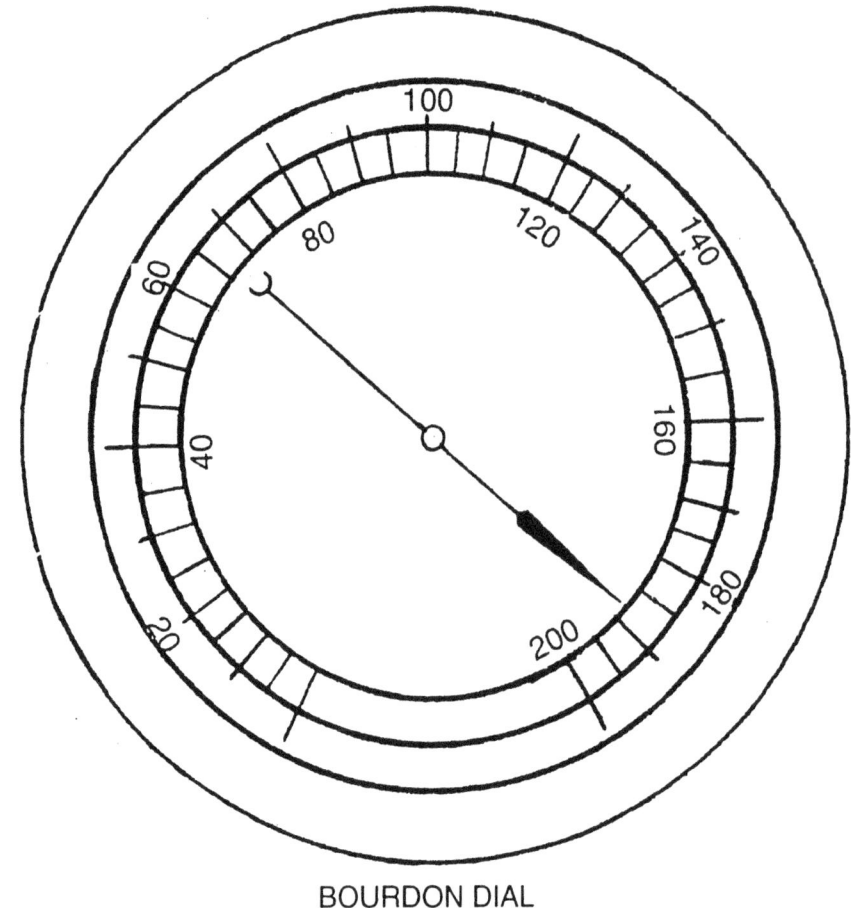

BOURDON DIAL

The reading indicated on the above dial is MOST NEARLY

A. 183   B. 188   C. 192   D. 196

17. An instrument used for detecting the sound of flowing water in a pipe network is a(n)

    A. micrometer   B. spectrometer
    C. aquaphone   D. viscophone

18. Of the following, the MAIN purpose of a Venturi meter is to measure the _____ in a main.

    A. quantity of water flowing
    B. chlorine content of the water
    C. velocity of the water
    D. temperature of the water

19. A blade with a small hole in the tip, used for measuring the flow from a hydrant, is a

    A. hydrant pitot   B. Venturi meter
    C. parshall flume   D. hydrant head

20. Hydrant-flow tests include observation of the pressure at a centrally situated hydrant and measurement of

    A. pressure at a group of neighboring hydrants
    B. flow from outlets at the top floor of a building
    C. reservoir elevation
    D. flow from a group of neighboring hydrants

21. Of the following, the one which is NOT a requirement of a satisfactory report is that it should be

    A. timely B. lengthy C. legible D. accurate

22. When an accident occurs, the FIRST concern of the Foreman should be to

    A. see that injured person is properly cared for
    B. make sketches of the area
    C. interview the injured person
    D. interview witnesses and coworkers

23. Workers whose characteristics and behavior are such as to make them considerably more liable to injury than the average person are considered to be

    A. late
    B. safety conscious
    C. careful
    D. accident-prone

24. Safety inspections are not useful in an accident prevention program unless

    A. all persons who have accidents are fined
    B. insurance rates are decreased
    C. immediate action is taken to correct the conditions revealed
    D. there is adequate compensation for all injured parties

25. A Foreman is BEST qualified to investigate accidents involving his subordinates because he

    A. has all safety equipment for the job
    B. has more free time than his superiors
    C. has more skill than his superiors
    D. is familiar with all the job conditions

KEY (CORRECT ANSWERS)

1.	C	11.	B
2.	D	12.	B
3.	C	13.	B
4.	C	14.	B
5.	B	15.	D
6.	B	16.	B
7.	C	17.	C
8.	C	18.	A
9.	A	19.	A
10.	A	20.	D

21. B
22. A
23. D
24. C
25. D

EXAMINATION SECTION
TEST 1

DIRECTIONS: Each question or incomplete statement is followed by several suggested answers or completions. Select the one that BEST answers the question or completes the statement. *PRINT THE LETTER OF THE CORRECT ANSWER IN THE SPACE AT THE RIGHT.*

Questions 1-5.

DIRECTIONS: Questions 1 through 5, inclusive, refer to the distribution map shown on the LAST page of this test. All questions are to be answered in accordance with this map.

1. The symbol just west of the boundary gate symbol on 21st Street between Willow Avenue and Meadow Avenue is a

    A. hydrant
    B. gate valve
    C. check valve
    D. reducer

2. The number of hydrants on the 30" main in Meadow Avenue between 22nd Street and 23rd Street is

    A. none   B. 1   C. 2   D. 3

3. The *S* symbol on the main at the west end of 18th Street means that the main is

    A. a special casting
    B. made of steel
    C. shut down
    D. high pressure service

4. A cap is located at or near the intersection of _____ Street and _____ Avenue.

    A. 24th; Willow
    B. 22nd; Willow
    C. 26th; Meadow
    D. 21st; Central

5. A blow off is located in

    A. Meadow Avenue between 19th & 20th Streets
    B. 22nd Street between Willow Avenue and Meadow Avenue
    C. Wilen Avenue between 22nd and 23rd Streets
    D. 22nd Street between Willow Avenue and Central Avenue

6. Assume that a normally sober man appears on the job intoxicated. Of the following, the BEST procedure for a foreman to follow is to

    A. give the man an easy job so that he cannot get hurt
    B. let the man *sleep it off* in the morning and put him to work in the afternoon
    C. let the man work at his normal duties but keep an *eye* on him
    D. send him home for the day

7. The Chief Engineer has decided to change the procedure that must be followed in making certain types of repairs. The one of the following statements concerning the new procedure that is CORRECT is:
The men

A. should know why the procedure is being changed because they will then be more interested in the job
B. do not have to know the reason for the change because they need do only the work as they are told
C. should know why the procedure is being changed so that they can decide which method of doing the job is better
D. do not have to know the reason for the change because they are not capable of judging the best method of doing a job

8. A foreman, by mistake, orders his men to do a job improperly.
Of the following, the BEST thing for the foreman to do when he realizes his error is to

A. insist that the job be done as he ordered so that his mistake will not be discovered
B. admit that he made the mistake and correct the order
C. tell the men that the order came from *higher up so* that he will not be blamed for the mistake
D. tell the men that he is merely trying this out to see if it works better

9. The BEST foreman is usually the

A. fastest worker
B. man who is most familiar with the streets in the borough
C. strongest man
D. man who is most tactful

10. A good foreman will

A. look after the welfare of his men
B. demand perfection in the work of his men at all times
C. make special efforts to impress his superiors
D. cover up for the actions of his men

11. As a newly appointed foreman, it is MOST important that you

A. show the men who is boss by issuing orders
B. prove to the men that you know more than they do
C. become acquainted with the men and their abilities
D. show the men how friendly you are

12. A foreman who criticizes his department head is a

A. *good* foreman, because the men will feel he is on their side
B. *poor* foreman, because the men will lose respect for him
C. *good* foreman, because he will get more work done
D. *poor* foreman, because he will have no time to do his own work

13. One of the men in your gang comes to you, the foreman, and complains that the men in the gang have taken a dislike to him and are making trouble for him.
Of the following, the BEST thing for you to do is to

A. tell the man he must learn to get along with the other men
B. report the matter to your superior
C. call the gang together and tell them they must stop making trouble
D. investigate the complaint to determine what the problem is

14. As a foreman, you are inspecting the damage done by water from a broken main leaking into the basement of a store. After inspecting the damage, the owner complains to you about the conduct of the men who made the repair.
Of the following, the BEST way of handling this situation is to tell the owner that

   A. you are there to inspect the damage to the premises only
   B. he should make his complaint to higher authorities
   C. his complaint will be investigated and, if found correct, proper action will be taken
   D. nothing can be done at this time since the men are no longer at this location

Questions 15-17.

DIRECTIONS: Questions 15 through 17, inclusive, are based on the paragraph below. These questions are to be answered in accordance with the information given in this paragraph.

Excavation of trench. The trench shall be excavated as directed; one side of the street or avenue shall be left open for traffic at all times. In paved streets, the length of trench that may be opened between the point where the backfilling has been completed and the point where the pavement is being removed shall not exceed fifteen hundred feet for pipes 24 inches or less in diameter. For pipes larger than 24 inch, the length of open trenches shall not exceed one thousand feet. The completion of the backfilling shall be interpreted to mean the backfilling of the trench and the consolidation of the backfill so that vehicular traffic can be resumed over the backfill, and also the placing of any temporary pavement that *may* be required.

15. According to the above paragraph, the street

   A. can be closed to traffic in emergencies
   B. can be closed to traffic only when laying more than 1500 feet of pipe
   C. is closed to traffic as directed
   D. shall be left open for traffic at all times

16. According to the above paragraph, the MAXIMUM length of open trench permitted in paved streets depends on the

   A. traffic on the street
   B. type of ground that is being excaVated
   C. water conditions met with in excavation
   D. diameter of the pipe being laid

17. According to the above paragraph, the one of the following items that is included in the *completion of the back-filling* is

   A. sheeting and bracing   B. cradle
   C. temporary pavement   D. bridging

Questions 18-20.

DIRECTIONS: Questions 18 through 20, inclusive, are based on the paragraph below. These questions are to be answered in accordance with the information given in this paragraph.

The Contractor shall notify the Engineer by noon of the day immediately preceding the date when he wishes to shut down any main, and if the time set be approved, the Contractor shall provide the men necessary to shut down the main at the time stipulated, and to previously notify all consumers whose supply may be affected. These men shall be under the direction of the Department employees, who will superintend all operations of valves and hydrants. Shutdowns for making connections will not be made unless and until the Contractor has everything on the ground in readiness for the work.

18. According to the above paragraph, before a contractor can make a shut-down, he MUST notify the

    A. Police Department
    B. district foreman
    C. engineer
    D. highway department

19. According to the above paragraph, the operation of the valves will be supervised by the

    A. department employees
    B. contractor's men
    C. contractor's superintendent
    D. engineer

20. According to the above paragraph, shut-downs for connections are made

    A. the day before the connection is made
    B. first and then consumers are notified
    C. at any time convenient to the contractor
    D. when the contractor has everything on the ground in readiness for the work

21. Water hammer in a pipe line is MOST frequently caused by _____ a valve too _____ .

    A. opening; rapidly
    B. opening; slowly
    C. closing; rapidly
    D. closing; slowly

22. In using a hacksaw, pressure should be applied to the hacksaw when

    A. pushing it
    B. pulling it
    C. pushing and pulling it
    D. either pushing or pulling, depending upon the way the cut is to be made

23. When cutting cast iron (other than pipe) with a hacksaw, the PROPER number of teeth per inch in the blade should be

    A. 14   B. 18   C. 24   D. 32

24. Concrete is a mixture of cement and

    A. lime, sand, and water
    B. sand and water
    C. sand and broken stone
    D. sand, broken stone, and water

25. The head of a cold chisel has mushroomed after considerable use. The BEST thing to do is

   A. continue to use it since mushrooming is normal
   B. throw it away
   C. send it to the shop for redressing
   D. use a file to restore the head to its original shape

26. A valve box cover has been covered with asphalt during a street repaving job. The BEST way to locate the valve is to use a

   A. geophone
   B. aquaphone
   C. distribution map and a tape
   D. probing bar

27. The number of cubic yards in a bin 4 feet by 8 feet by 13 feet is MOST NEARLY _____ cubic yards.

   A. 17   B. 15   C. 13   D. 11

28. The letter *P* stencilled on the roadside face of a hydrant indicates that the hydrant

   A. is a low pressure hydrant
   B. is a high pressure hydrant
   C. is out of service permanently
   D. has a plugged drain

29. A hydrant extension piece would MOST likely be used if

   A. the hydrant had been damaged
   B. an open trench exists in the street in front of the hydrant
   C. several hose lines must be connected to the hydrant
   D. the hose connections do not fit the hydrant nozzles

30. The drip valve of a hydrant

   A. should not open until after the hydrant valve has closed
   B. should open just before the hydrant valve has closed
   C. operates completely independent of the operation of the hydrant valve
   D. should only be closed during repair of the hydrant

31. To remove and replace the operating parts of a hydrant which is in service,

   A. the standpipe must be disconnected from the elbow
   B. it is necessary to do some excavating
   C. the main must be shut down
   D. no excavation is necessary

32. The material generally used for packing hydrant stems is

   A. asbestos   B. rubber cloth
   C. flax   D. leather

33. A roundabout would normally have as a component part a

   A. four-way B. valve C. plug D. cap

34. Cast iron reducers are usually made in all but one of the following ways. The way in which they are NOT made is

   A. spigots on both ends
   B. hub on large end, spigot on small end
   C. hub on small end, spigot on large end
   D. hubs on both ends

35. A cast iron main running due east is to turn so that it runs N45W, that is, halfway between north and west. The change in direction could be made using _____ bends.

   A. sixteen 1/48 B. six 1/16
   C. four 1/8 D. two 1/4

36. A cast iron offset would NORMALLY be used

   A. to change the direction of a main
   B. when the main must run diagonally from one side of the street to the other
   C. when the main must be shifted parallel to itself several feet to avoid an existing structure
   D. when the main must be shifted several inches to avoid an existing structure

37. A 30-inch cast iron main is to be laid with a blow-off and an air cock. The cast iron piece used for the blow-off differs from that used for the air cock in

   A. size of outlet
   B. general shape
   C. material used
   D. length measured along the main

38. The upper part of a standard hydrant valve box is USUALLY connected to the lower part by

   A. screw threads B. bolts
   C. a beaded rim D. lugs and rods

39. A trench for an 18-inch cast iron main is being excavated in rock. The width of the trench should be AT LEAST _____ inches.

   A. 30 B. 36 C. 42 D. 48

40. Specifications of the Department of Water Supply, Gas and Electricity state that in a trench excavated in rock, projections of rock must be removed if they come within a certain distance of the outside of any portion of the pipe barrel or bell. This distance is, in inches,

   A. 4 B. 6 C. 8 D. 10

KEY (CORRECT ANSWERS)

1.	D	11.	C	21.	C	31.	D
2.	A	12.	B	22.	A	32.	C
3.	B	13.	D	23.	B	33.	B
4.	D	14.	C	24.	D	34.	D
5.	D	15.	D	25.	C	35.	B
6.	D	16.	D	26.	C	36.	D
7.	A	17.	C	27.	B	37.	A
8.	B	18.	C	28.	D	38.	A
9.	D	19.	A	29.	B	39.	C
10.	A	20.	D	30.	A	40.	B

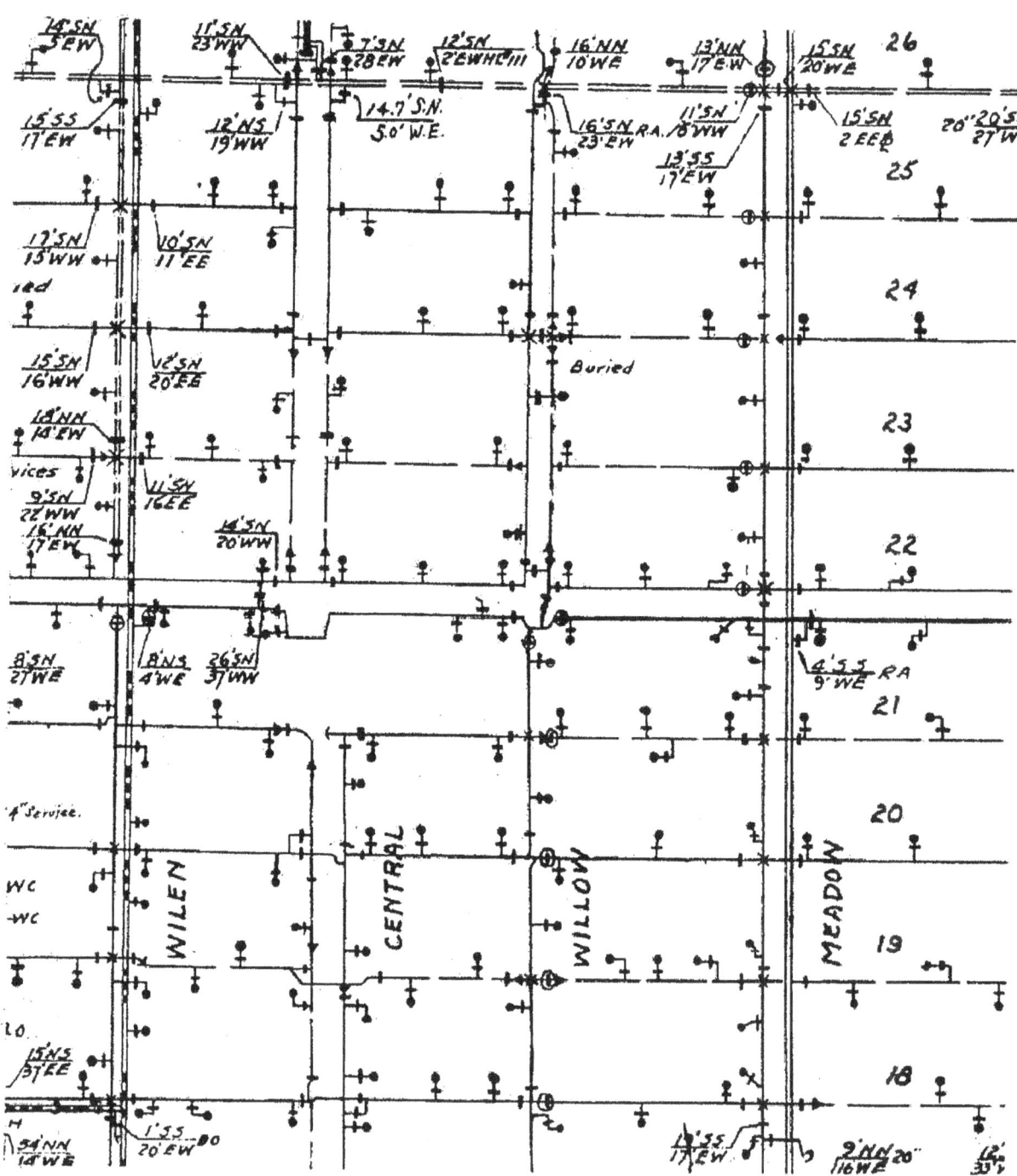

TEST 2

DIRECTIONS: Each question or incomplete statement is followed by several suggested answers or completions. Select the one that BEST answers the question or completes the statement. *PRINT THE LETTER OF THE CORRECT ANSWER IN THE SPACE AT THE RIGHT.*

1. The MAXIMUM size of stones permitted in backfill is _____ inches.

    A. 12   B. 8   C. 4   D. 2

2. A two-inch galvanized steel pipe is to be connected to a cast iron main.
   The connection should be made by a standard corporation tap of the following size: _____ inch.

    A. 1   B. 1 1/2   C. 2   D. 2 1/2

3. Standard cast iron pipe of inside diameter from 12 to 20 inches may be furnished in nominal laying lengths up to and including _____ feet.

    A. 14   B. 16   C. 18   D. 20

4. The interior surface of new 12-inch cast iron pipe is USUALLY coated with

    A. cement mortar   B. nothing
    C. asphalt paint   D. coal tar pitch

5. A tarpaulin would MOST likely be used when

    A. mixing concrete
    B. running lead joints
    C. lowering pipe into a trench
    D. excavating a trench for a water main

6. Bands and bolts would be LEAST likely to be required at

    A. bends   B. branches   C. plugs   D. four-ways

7. A house service with a 3/8-inch tap on an existing main is to be transferred to a new main.
   The size of the tap on the new main should be _____ inch.

    A. 5/8   B. 1/2   C. 3/8   D. 1/4

8. The LARGEST tap permitted on a new 12-inch main is _____ inch.

    A. 1   B. 1 1/2   C. 2   D. 2 1/2

9. The sheeting of a trench serves

    A. only to protect workmen
    B. only to prevent damage to existing mains close to the trench
    C. only to prevent damage to pavement
    D. all three of the foregoing purposes

10. Water required for flushing backfill is USUALLY supplied

    A. in a fine spray
    B. by an ordinary garden hose
    C. from a tank truck
    D. through a flushing pipe

11. Water mains are USUALLY laid parallel to the curb at a distance of APPROXIMATELY _____ feet.

    A. 15   B. 12   C. 9   D. 6

12. After a main has been laid but prior to putting it into service, it should be disinfected by

    A. continuous flushing with water containing chlorine
    B. continuous flushing with clean water only
    C. introducing chlorine into the water in the pipe and letting the solution stand for 30 minutes
    D. blowing chlorine gas through the main

13. Before trimming a caulked pipe joint, the lead of a lead joint should

    A. extend outside the face of the bell
    B. be flush with the face of the bell
    C. be inside the face of the bell
    D. be heated

14. Drainage of hydrants require the use of lead lined pipe

    A. except when a cast iron drain base is provided
    B. except when the hydrant is connected to a sewer
    C. except when a blind drain is provided
    D. in every case

15. A standard cast iron reducer is to connect a 24-inch main to a smaller main. The length of the reducer USUALLY

    A. is the same regardless of the size of the smaller main
    B. decreases as the size of the smaller main decreases
    C. increases as the size of the smaller main decreases
    D. can be varied to fit the field conditions

16. A standard cast iron three-way does NOT have more than the following number of hubs:

    A. 3   B. 2   C. 1   D. 0

17. Of the following statements, the one which is CORRECT is:

    A. A cap is used on the spigot end of a pipe
    B. A plug is used on the spigot end of a pipe
    C. Caps and plugs can be used interchangeably
    D. Caps are usually available in larger sizes than plugs

18. Of the following statements, the one which is CORRECT is:

    A. A planned shutdown is not made rapidly
    B. In the event of an emergency shutdown, all valves in the area should be closed and then a study of the distribution map should be made to determine which valves can be opened
    C. Boundary gates should always be kept closed for the duration of an emergency shutdown
    D. The operation of all valves to be used in a planned shutdown should be checked prior to making the shutdown

19. When building material is stored on the street for the construction of a building,

    A. the Department of Water Supply, Gas and Electricity is not concerned
    B. there can be no objections if hydrants are accessible
    C. there can be no objections if the storage period is short
    D. serious difficulties for the Department of Water Supply, Gas and Electricity could result

20. A large steel main is to be emptied through a blow-off. The BEST way to proceed is to open

    A. the blow-off
    B. an aircock or hydrant at the high point of the main before opening the blow-off
    C. the blow-off and then open an air cock or hydrant at the high point of the main
    D. an air cock or hydrant at the low point of the main before opening the blow-off

21. A large new main is to be placed in service.
    To fill the main, it is important to FIRST open

    A. the head gate valve
    B. an air cock or hydrant on the main
    C. all side gate valves
    D. the side gate valves on one side of the main only

22. Of the following special castings, the one which is MOST like a blow-off is a

    A. four-way   B. reducer   C. three-way   D. offset

23. The laying length of a double hub

    A. is less than one foot
    B. depends upon the diameter of the pipe
    C. must be at least nine feet
    D. may be any length up to 20 feet, the maximum length depending upon the diameter

24. The gooseneck that is GENERALLY used to connect a service pipe to a main

    A. should be straight for its entire length
    B. comes in a standard length and, therefore, must be curved to make it fit

C. is deliberately curved so that it can accommodate movement between main and service pipe
D. is curved to provide extra length so that it can be cut and still be long enough to reconnect to the main

25. A non-rising stem gate valve would MOST likely be used when

    A. the threads of the stem must be readily accessible for lubrication
    B. space is limited
    C. the valve is used infrequently
    D. the valve is in a deep valve vault

26. Of the following types of valves, the one which is NOT usually found on water mains is the _____ valve.

    A. glove   B. air relief
    C. pressure regulating   D. gate

27. When a length of cast iron pipe is too long, it is USUALLY cut with a(n)

    A. chisel   B. hacksaw
    C. emery wheel   D. cutting torch

28. The PRINCIPAL objection to laying mains between December 15 and March 15 is with the

    A. freezing of water
    B. working conditions for the men
    C. freezing of soil
    D. the reduced length of daylight

29. A trench for a cast iron main is USUALLY backfilled immediately

    A. after the joints are caulked
    B. after the pressure test has been completed
    C. before water is placed in the main
    D. after water is placed in the main

30. When the pavement along the sides of a trench becomes undermined, the BEST thing to do is

    A. carefully tamp the backfill under the undermined pavement
    B. place a layer of broken stone on top of the backfill under the undermined pavement
    C. break down the undermined pavement before backfilling
    D. consolidate the backfill by thorough flushing

31. A small leak in a main would usually be MOST serious in the

    A. summer   B. fall   C. spring   D. winter

32. When sheeting for a trench is not to be removed before backfilling, the sheeting should be driven or cut off so that it

    A. is flush with the surface of the ground
    B. is at least 8 inches below the surface of the ground

C. will project at least two inches into the pavement base
D. is flush with the top surface of the pavement base

33. While excavating a trench in rock by blasting, a water main which crosses the line of the trench is uncovered. Of the following methods, the BEST one for continuing the rock excavation in the vicinity of the main is

   A. shut down the main
   B. place blasting mats to cover the main
   C. use lighter blasting charges
   D. relocate the main temporarily so that it is outside the danger area of the building

34. When the bottom of a trench for a water main is in rock, the pipe should be permanently supported on

   A. clean earth backfill which is tamped
   B. wooden blocking
   C. sand backfill which is flushed
   D. concreted cradles

35. On which one of the following days of the week should a planned shutdown normally be made?

   A. Sunday
   B. Monday
   C. Tuesday
   D. Wednesday

36. Permissible leakage during a field test is two (2) gallons per linear foot of pipe joint per 24 hours.
   For a 24-inch main, 1,000 feet long, with 16-foot laying lengths, the permissible leakage in 24 hours is, in gallons, MOST NEARLY

   A. 750 B. 770 C. 790 D. 810

37. Contract limitations on the maximum quantities of materials that may be delivered to the site, and on the time of such deliveries, are USUALLY made in order to

   A. insure the completion of the work on schedule
   B. prevent the contractor from asking for an extension of time because materials were not available
   C. reduce congestion at the site of the work
   D. protect the manufacturer supplying the material

38. Steel reinforcing bars for reinforced concrete should

   A. be painted with red lead
   B. be painted with asphalt paint
   C. be painted with oil paint
   D. not be painted

39. Steel water mains are lined with

   A. coal tar enamel only
   B. coal tar enamel or cement mortar
   C. cement mortar only
   D. nothing

40. The principal danger in NOT opening an air cock when draining a main is that the main might   40_____

   A. not empty
   B. only partly empty
   C. empty too fast
   D. collapse

KEY (CORRECT ANSWERS)

1. C	11. C	21. B	31. D
2. B	12. A	22. C	32. B
3. D	13. A	23. A	33. D
4. A	14. D	24. C	34. D
5. C	15. C	25. B	35. D
6. D	16. B	26. A	36. C
7. A	17. A	27. A	37. C
8. C	18. D	28. C	38. D
9. D	19. D	29. A	39. B
10. D	20. B	30. C	40. D

EXAMINATION SECTION
TEST 1

DIRECTIONS: Each question or incomplete statement is followed by several suggested answers or completions. Select the one that BEST answers the question or completes the statement. *PRINT THE LETTER OF THE CORRECT ANSWER IN THE SPACE AT THE RIGHT.*

1. If cast iron weighs 450 pounds per cubic foot, the weight of a solid cast iron manhole cover 2 feet in diameter and 1 inch thick is MOST NEARLY _____ pounds.

    A. 94   B. 118   C. 136   D. 164

    1._____

2. A gas which has an odor similar to rotten eggs is

    A. argon
    B. phosgene
    C. nitrogen
    D. hydrogen sulfide

    2._____

3. The gases released by digesting sewage sludges contain about 72%

    A. methane   B. chlorine   C. helium   D. copper

    3._____

4. In sewer maintenance, an orange peel bucket is USUALLY used for

    A. testing for toxic gases
    B. rodding sewers
    C. cleaning roof drains
    D. cleaning catch basins

    4._____

5. A plumbing device that prevents the passage of bad odors and gases from the sewer system to a building is a

    A. corporation stop
    B. union
    C. curb box
    D. trap

    5._____

6. An 8-inch diameter sewer enters at the upstream side of a manhole, and a 10-inch sewer leaves at the downstream side. The crowns of the sewers are at the same elevation. If the invert elevation of the 8-inch sewer is 100.64 feet, the invert elevation of the 10-inch sewer is MOST NEARLY _____ feet.

    A. 100.32   B. 100.41   C. 100.47   D. 100.52

    6._____

7. Where ground slopes are unfavorable, it is necessary to keep sanitary sewer grades at the minimum velocity that will prevent the settling of material when the sewer is flowing full.
   The velocity is MOST NEARLY _____ feet per second.

    A. 0.2   B. 2.0   C. 20.0   D. 200.0

    7._____

8. A condition that will permit polluted water to enter a potable water supply is a

    A. tide gate
    B. cross connection
    C. cathodic protection
    D. reducer

    8._____

9. A wheel with a grooved rim, such as is mounted in a pulley block to guide rope or cable, is a

    A. turnbuckle
    B. wormgear
    C. slant
    D. sheave

    9._____

10. A device used in a combined sewer to bypass excess storm-flow is a(n)

    A. soffit
    B. side-flow weir
    C. aquafer
    D. cellular cofferdam

11. A device installed at the discharge end of a sewer outfall which operates to permit gravity flow at low stages in the receiving waters, but closes to prevent backflow when the elevation of the receiving waters is high, is a

    A. flume
    B. buttress
    C. tide gate
    D. flocculator

12. A pipe used to carry streamflow under a highway embankment is a

    A. culvert B. lock C. standpipe D. pitot

13. The pipe on the discharge side of a sewage pump is a

    A. tell-tale pipe
    B. sump pipe
    C. suction pipe
    D. force main

14. A model 6520 sewer cleaner is rated at 60 GPM at 1000 PSI. As used here, PSI is an abbreviation for

    A. positive surging inflow
    B. per sewer invert
    C. pounds per square inch
    D. pounds per sewer inlet

15. In order to increase culvert efficiency and to prevent undermining of the culvert, the entrance to the culvert is FREQUENTLY provided with a

    A. sump pump
    B. mud valve
    C. head wall
    D. scroll case

16. A sewer plan calls for pipe diameters of 3", 10", 12", 14", 15", and 18". The size which is NOT used for a standard strength clay sewer pipe is

    A. 10" B. 12" C. 14" D. 15"

17. Lateral sanitary sewers should PREFERABLY intersect at a

    A. catch basin
    B. weir
    C. manhole
    D. tide gate

18. A dip, or sag, used in a sewer line to pass under structures, such as subways, is called a(n)

    A. outfall
    B. inverted siphon
    C. force main
    D. regulator

19. A device suitable for pumping sewage from deep basements into city sewers is a

    A. pressure relief valve
    B. vacuum breaker
    C. pneumatic ejector
    D. comminutor

20. The flow of ground water into sanitary sewers through defective joints is called

    A. back siphonage
    B. infiltration
    C. overflow
    D. exfiltration

KEY (CORRECT ANSWERS)

1. B
2. D
3. A
4. D
5. D

6. C
7. B
8. B
9. D
10. B

11. C
12. A
13. D
14. C
15. C

16. C
17. C
18. B
19. C
20. B

TEST 2

DIRECTIONS: Each question or incomplete statement is followed by several suggested answers or completions. Select the one that BEST answers the question or completes the statement. *PRINT THE LETTER OF THE CORRECT ANSWER IN THE SPACE AT THE RIGHT.*

1. In a combined sewer system, the amount of sewage flowing to the treatment plant is USUALLY controlled by a 1._____

    A. regulator
    B. bar screen
    C. siphon
    D. mud valve

2. The LOWEST portion of the inside of a sewer pipe is the 2._____

    A. crown
    B. haunch
    C. invert
    D. spring line

3. A.C. pipe, sometimes used instead of clay sewer pipe, is made of 3._____

    A. reinforced concrete
    B. polyvinyl
    C. asbestos and cement
    D. asphalt

4. Of the following, the one which is NOT a sewer cleaning tool is the 4._____

    A. gouge
    B. wire brush
    C. pilaster
    D. claw

5. A sewer rodding machine has speeds up to 100 FPM. As used here, FPM is an abbreviation for feet per 5._____

    A. million   B. mile   C. minute   D. module

6. The nominal diameter of a #4 reinforcing bar is MOST NEARLY 6._____

    A. 0.4"   B. 0.04"   C. 0.5"   D. 4 mm

7. In a 1:2:3 concrete mix, the number 3 represents the proportion of 7._____

    A. sand
    B. water
    C. coarse aggregate
    D. cement

8. Of the following, a procedure used for causing air to flow into and from the lungs of the body by mechanical or manual methods is called 8._____

    A. irrigation
    B. traction
    C. traumatic shock
    D. artificial respiration

9. The one of the following that is a toxic gas which is colorless and odorless is 9._____

    A. chlorine
    B. hydrogen sulfide
    C. carbon monoxide
    D. gasoline

10. In first aid, a tourniquet is MOST often used to 10._____

    A. improve respiration
    B. treat burns
    C. treat sprains
    D. control bleeding

11. Persons who have been injured may suffer a depressed condition of many of the body functions due to failure of enough blood to circulate through the body.
    This condition is called

    A. immunization
    B. chronic
    C. cathartic
    D. shock

11.____

12. The type of injury which is MOST likely to cause lockjaw (tetanus) is

    A. an epileptic convulsion
    B. a puncture wound
    C. an electric shock
    D. sunstroke

12.____

13. Wellpoints are used in sewer construction PRIMARILY to

    A. remove gases
    B. dewater trenches
    C. locate wells
    D. replace hydrants

13.____

14. A sewer which carries only sewage from the plumbing fixtures in a house is a

    A. storm sewer
    B. combined sewer
    C. sanitary sewer
    D. subsurface drain

14.____

15. The slope of a sewer is MOST usually indicated by the units,

    A. feet
    B. rods
    C. percent
    D. diameters

15.____

16. Longitudinal timbers used to support the vertical sheeting in a sewer trench excavation are called

    A. wales
    B. cross braces
    C. piles
    D. cradles

16.____

17. The sum of 2 5/8, 3 3/16, 1 1/2, and 4 1/4 is

    A. 9 13/16
    B. 10 7/16
    C. 11 9/16
    D. 13 3/16

17.____

Questions 18-20.

DIRECTIONS: Questions 18 through 20 should be answered by selecting the word that MOST NEARLY means the SAME as the word in capital letters.

18. SUPPLEMENT

    A. terminal
    B. absence
    C. addition
    D. void

18.____

19. HAZARDOUS

    A. dense
    B. safe
    C. dangerous
    D. high

19.____

20. VERIFY

    A. climb
    B. travel
    C. slide
    D. confirm

20.____

KEY (CORRECT ANSWERS)

1. A
2. C
3. C
4. C
5. C
6. C
7. C
8. D
9. C
10. D
11. D
12. B
13. B
14. C
15. C
16. A
17. C
18. C
19. C
20. D

EXAMINATION SECTION
TEST 1

DIRECTIONS: Each question or incomplete statement is followed by several suggested answers or completions. Select the one that BEST answers the question or completes the statement. *PRINT THE LETTER OF THE CORRECT ANSWER IN THE SPACE AT THE RIGHT.*

1. Assume that a foreman has a new assistant.
Of the following, the BEST thing for the foreman to do FIRST in order to prepare his assistant to help him with his work and to take over in his absence is to

    A. tell the men that they must give full cooperation to his assistant
    B. assign one of his duties to his assistant and follow-up to see if he does it well
    C. let his assistant know as much as possible about everything he is doing or planning
    D. discuss all matters with his assistant before taking any action

    1.____

2. Of the following, the MOST important reason for the foreman to insist that his workers follow good housekeeping practices is that

    A. a neat and orderly work area will make the foreman look good to his superiors
    B. such tasks represent a good way of keeping the men busy after they have completed their regular assignments
    C. neatness in the working environment will raise the men's morale
    D. good housekeeping is an important element in accident prevention

    2.____

3. Supervising a lazy worker is often very difficult, especially if he is a likeable and capable person.
Of the following ways a foreman might deal with such a worker, the one which would be LEAST effective in improving his performance would be to

    A. supervise him closely so that the worker will not have the opportunity to neglect his work
    B. give him a job with some responsibility in the hope that this will motivate him to a greater effort
    C. give him unpleasant jobs in order to get him to change his work habits
    D. give him, in a private conference, a firm warning that his laziness cannot be tolerated

    3.____

4. A good foreman supervises his crew completely, even if this means doing some of their work if he can do it better. This statement is GENERALLY

    A. *true*, mainly because a foreman should not make his crew do tasks that he would not do himself
    B. *false*, mainly because the foreman who does this damages his workers' attitude toward the job
    C. *true*, mainly because by watching the foreman the workers can learn how to do a better job
    D. *false*, mainly because the foreman does not have time to do work other than his own

    4.____

5. Assume that you, as foreman, read a new department policy to your employees. Later, you find that they did not understand the policy.
   Of the following, the BEST thing for you to do next is to

   A. have the men read the policy and initial it after they read it
   B. write up and distribute an explanation of the policy among the men
   C. arrange a session to explain the policy and allow time for the men to discuss it with you
   D. ask your supervisor to explain the policy to the workers

6. Assume that, as foreman, you find that one of your men is going about a job in the wrong way.
   In criticizing this worker, you should

   A. add some words or phrases to soften the blow while telling him specifically what he is doing wrong
   B. try to be as general as possible so as to spare the feelings of the worker
   C. criticize him strongly and threaten him with disciplinary action so that he won't fall into a habit of making such mistakes
   D. allow him to see the effects of his mistakes so that the criticism will appear justified and well-deserved

7. For you, as a foreman, to issue written instructions to your men when they have a complicated job to do would be desirable, CHIEFLY because when the men are following written instructions

   A. they can work more quickly
   B. they are less likely to make serious errors in the work
   C. the need for you to inspect the work that they have done would be eliminated
   D. they do not have to make any decisions on their own

8. The training of new workers is one of the foreman's most important tasks.
   In order to introduce a new employee correctly to his job, the one of the following actions a foreman should take FIRST is to

   A. show the new employee the details of his job
   B. explain to the new employee the overall purpose of his job
   C. let the new employee start working on his own, helping him when he asks for it
   D. ask the new employee what type of assignment he would like most

9. Assume that a foreman has assigned an assistant foreman the responsibility for supervising a job.
   Of the following, it is MOST important for him to

   A. give the assistant foreman close supervision to keep him from making obvious mistakes
   B. tell the assistant foreman what jobs to assign to the men who will work with him
   C. give the assistant foreman the authority to make necessary decisions and give orders
   D. require frequent progress reports from the assistant foreman

10. One of the duties of a foreman is to check the work of his men as it progresses. Of the following, the BEST reason for a foreman to inspect work periodically is to

    A. develop standard work procedures
    B. check that the work is being done in the most efficient manner
    C. eliminate the necessity for a final inspection
    D. watch for slow workers and assign them to other jobs

11. As a foreman, you may find it necessary to obtain the approval of your superior before you take action on some matters.
    Of the following, the action for which it is MOST important that you obtain such approval is one that involves

    A. transferring one of your functions from your unit to another unit
    B. rotating assignments among your men
    C. putting one of your men in charge when you expect to be out for a day
    D. disciplining two men who have had a fight on the job

12. Some foremen issue assignments in the form of requests rather than giving direct orders. This practice is GENERALLY

    A. *poor*, mainly because issuing a request leaves it up to the worker to set the time when he will do the task
    B. *good*, mainly because requesting the worker to do a job permits him to use judgment in deciding how to do the job
    C. *poor*, mainly because requests carry less weight than direct orders and imply weakness on the part of the foreman
    D. *good*, mainly because requests carry almost the same weight as a direct order and are less likely to offend the worker

13. Assume that, as a newly appointed foreman, you find that the stock distribution system in your shop is unsatisfactory and you decide to change it. You then put into effect a new system which totally changes the old system. This kind of move is USUALLY

    A. *undesirable*, chiefly because any new system should use the good features of the old system as far as possible
    B. *desirable*, chiefly because attempts to combine features of an old system with those of a new system usually do not work out
    C. *undesirable*, chiefly because you should not throw out the old system until you prove that the new one is better
    D. *desirable*, chiefly because it is always easier to establish a new system than to change an old one

14. Assume that you are a foreman and that a new worker in your crew has made an error which resulted in injury to another man.
    Of the following, the MOST important thing you should do about this incident is to

    A. have the new worker assigned to different work where accidents are less likely
    B. study the accident and plan ways of preventing similar accidents
    C. talk with your entire work crew about the importance of proper safety procedures
    D. tell the other workers in your crew to be especially careful when working with the new man

15. The BEST way for a foreman to keep morale high among his men is to   15._____

    A. give the good workers the best jobs
    B. praise the men when they do a good job
    C. individually assist the men on all their jobs
    D. grant special privileges to those doing good work

16. When a foreman arrives at a job location, he finds that a loud argument is going on   16._____
    between two of his men.
    He should FIRST

    A. send one of the men to another job
    B. find out what caused the argument before deciding what to do
    C. ask one of the other men to tell him the cause of the argument
    D. take the men with him to his boss so that the matter can be settled

17. Assume that you have recently been appointed foreman. Several of the men in your   17._____
    gang, who are good friends of yours, are taking advantage of the situation by slowing
    down in their work.
    As a foreman, you should FIRST

    A. let it ride since they will probably come around eventually
    B. request that these men be transferred out of your gang
    C. tell them that they must do their work on time
    D. write a note to your boss about what they are doing so that he can take action

18. The BEST action for a foreman to take if one of his men makes a suggestion on how to   18._____
    improve a work procedure is to

    A. listen to the suggestion and then let the man know as soon as possible if the suggestion can be used
    B. use the suggestion without naming the man who made it since the others in the gang might resent it
    C. tell the man the suggestion is good but say nothing further if you do not think it will work
    D. inform your boss of the suggestion but don't mention the man's name to avoid embarrassing him if the suggestion is turned down

19. The BEST thing for a foreman to do when a new rule comes down from the top which he   19._____
    feels will be unpopular with the men is to

    A. simply inform the men of the rule without commenting on it
    B. explain the reason for the new rule
    C. announce the rule and tell the men no changes from it will be permitted
    D. explain to the men that he disagrees with the rule, but he can do nothing about it

20. You notice that another foreman is allowing his men to use defective equipment which   20._____
    may eventually result in unnecessary costs and perhaps injury to his men.
    The BEST thing for you, as a foreman, to do is to

    A. discuss the matter with your boss
    B. speak to the other foreman about the matter
    C. speak to the men who are using the unsafe equipment and have them talk to their foreman about the matter
    D. mind your own business and do not interfere with the other foreman

21. Of the following, the one thing that would MOST likely weaken the authority of a foreman in the eyes of his men would be

    A. posting a minimum number of rules
    B. periodically reviewing the accepted standards of work and conduct
    C. willingness to listen to suggestions from any of the men
    D. a policy of consulting with his boss on nearly all matters which are of a routine nature

22. Assume that you, as a foreman, have told one of your men how to do a certain job. On a day when you were absent, your boss comes in to check on the job and gives the man different orders.
    Of the following, it would be BEST for you to

    A. discuss the matter privately with your boss
    B. tell the man that he should have told your boss to see you first
    C. check with your boss before giving orders in the future
    D. tell the men that in the future your orders must be followed without any changes

23. Before a foreman recommends that charges be preferred against one of his men for breaking the rules, the foreman should FIRST make absolutely sure that

    A. the charges will be sustained at the hearing
    B. he has all the necessary information on the case
    C. his boss will approve the recommendation
    D. the man's fellow workers will give testimony favorable to the foreman's side of the case

24. The BEST way for a foreman to handle a complaint which has little merit is for the foreman to FIRST

    A. start it through the standard grievance procedure
    B. acknowledge the complaint but take no action
    C. warn the man that complaints of this sort make him subject to ridicule
    D. discuss the complaint with the man, pointing out its weakness

25. After having been instructed by your boss how to do a special rush job, you are forced, by unforeseen difficulties, to change the method without having time to check with the boss. When the boss inspects the job, he criticizes you for not doing what he told you.
    As a foreman, it would be BEST for you to

    A. complain to the boss's superior
    B. explain the situation to the boss
    C. say nothing but continue to do the job your way after the boss leaves
    D. tell the boss that he is to blame because he was not around when needed

KEY (CORRECT ANSWERS)

1.	C	11.	A
2.	D	12.	D
3.	C	13.	A
4.	B	14.	B
5.	C	15.	B
6.	A	16.	B
7.	B	17.	C
8.	B	18.	A
9.	C	19.	B
10.	B	20.	B

21. D
22. A
23. B
24. D
25. B

TEST 2

DIRECTIONS: Each question or incomplete statement is followed by several suggested answers or completions. Select the one that BEST answers the question or completes the statement. *PRINT THE LETTER OF THE CORRECT ANSWER IN THE SPACE AT THE RIGHT.*

1. Assume that one of the men asks his foreman to check every step of every job he completes. If the foreman feels that the only reason the man does this is to keep himself *in the clear*, the foreman should

    A. check every job in detail in order to protect himself
    B. refuse to check his work because as a foreman that is his right
    C. avoid the situation by telling the man that he has no time to check the work
    D. tell the man frankly that he is expected to accept some responsibility for what he does.

    1.____

2. Assume that one of a foreman's generally reliable men has been doing poor work lately. The BEST thing for the foreman to do FIRST would be to

    A. ask the man whether anything is wrong
    B. tell the man to snap out of it or disciplinary action will be taken
    C. remind the man that he can be brought up on charges
    D. mention that the boss has noticed the man's poor work and doesn't like it

    2.____

3. Assume that a new procedure is to be used in carrying out a certain job.
    The foreman should closely supervise the men using this new procedure in order to

    A. get the work done as quickly as possible
    B. impress his men with the importance of the job
    C. prevent his men from criticizing the new procedure
    D. make certain that his men are familiar with and understand all the details

    3.____

4. Good housekeeping in the foreman's work area will CHIEFLY depend upon the

    A. nature of the job
    B. skill of the men assigned
    C. quality of the supervision that the men receive
    D. quality of the material and equipment used

    4.____

5. A contractor doing a job for your agency demands to see your boss after accusing you of being prejudiced against him.
    The BEST of the following courses of action for you to follow is to

    A. take him to your boss as he requests
    B. ask him to leave your office if you feel that you are not prejudiced
    C. talk to him until you convince him you are not prejudiced
    D. remind him that you can make trouble for him if he fails to show you proper respect

    5.____

6. Of the following courses of action, the BEST one for a foreman to take if one of his men violates a minor safety rule is to

    A. request the rest of the gang to keep an eye on the man
    B. explain to the man how small mistakes can cause serious accidents
    C. point out to the man the only way he will learn is by making mistakes
    D. tell the man that everyone makes small mistakes and not to get upset about it

    6.____

7. Employees of an agency should regularly read the bulletin board at their job location MAINLY in order to

    A. learn about any changes in the staff of the agency
    B. learn what previously posted material has been removed
    C. become familiar with new orders and procedures posted on it
    D. show that they have an interest in the business of the agency

8. Assume that a foreman has just told one of his men how he wants a certain job done. Of the following, the BEST way to make sure that the man knows exactly how the foreman wants the job done is for the foreman to

    A. cross-examine the man
    B. repeat the instructions
    C. reword the instructions
    D. have the man tell him what has to be done and how

9. Your boss complains to you that he could not find you at your assigned location and that the gang under your supervision was idle while you were away.
Of the following, it is MOST important for you to

    A. improve your supervisory practices
    B. explain why you were away
    C. disregard such an unreasonable complaint
    D. make certain you are rarely away from your assigned location

10. A worker does not fully understand his foreman's instructions and asks for further explanation.
This is

    A. *not desirable;* the foreman's time will be wasted for no reason
    B. *not desirable;* the worker should be able to understand simple instructions
    C. *desirable;* the foreman will be impressed with the worker's interest
    D. *desirable;* proper performance depends on full understanding of the work to be done

11. Most people like to show what they can do.
Of the following, the job situation where a man would find it MOST difficult to demonstrate his skills and prove his competence is one where

    A. the work is challenging
    B. he is supervised too closely by his foreman
    C. his fellow workers possess the same basic skills as he does
    D. he is called upon frequently to learn new techniques and to operate new equipment

12. The BEST of the following reasons why a foreman should be familiar with first aid methods is that

    A. someone must be prepared to act quickly in an emergency
    B. the agency may be kept out of a lawsuit if a simple injury is taken care of promptly
    C. money is saved if someone can take care of simple injuries that do not require a doctor
    D. it is sometimes better to do the wrong thing than to do nothing in administering first aid

13. Assume that a foreman is preparing a report recommending that a standard work procedure be changed.
Of the following, the MOST important information that he should include in this report is

    A. a complete description of the present procedure
    B. the details and advantages of the recommended procedure
    C. the type and amount of retraining needed
    D. the percentage of men who favor the change

14. Of the following, the job that is BEST for a foreman to delegate to one of his men is one that

    A. is routine
    B. he finds disagreeable
    C. is of a policy-making nature
    D. occupies the greatest percentage of his time

15. Assume that you, the foreman, have been told by your boss that he has discovered a serious mistake on one of the jobs that you are in charge of.
The BEST action for you to take is to

    A. tell the boss promptly which one of the men made the mistake
    B. see that the man who made the mistake is not given similar work
    C. accept responsibility for the mistake and correct it
    D. explain that the mistake was made because you have so many new men

16. If a new man frequently reports late for work, his foreman should

    A. warn him privately that lateness will not be tolerated
    B. have him dropped at the end of his probation period
    C. threaten to transfer him if he continues to come in late
    D. embarrass him in front of the gang so he will break this habit

17. Advance planning of *fill-in* work for his men is helpful to a foreman MAINLY because he can use it to

    A. justify a request for more help
    B. show his men the need for speeding up the regular work
    C. prove to his boss that his men do not loaf on the job
    D. keep his men occupied whenever the regular work is delayed

18. The GREATEST advantage of rotating job assignments among the members of a foreman's crew is that rotation

    A. develops workers capable of handling many jobs
    B. insures a full day's work for each man
    C. determines what men are unable to learn new jobs
    D. equalizes the work load

19. A foreman assigning jobs to a group of new workers who have just finished a training course should GENERALLY assign these men to

   A. unimportant jobs since the new workers will probably make mistakes
   B. easy tasks so that the workers will develop a feeling of confidence
   C. jobs normally assigned to more skillful men so that they may learn more quickly
   D. difficult jobs in order to find out how many skills they have learned

20. Assume that a worker asks his foreman a question about a new maintenance procedure. The foreman is not thoroughly familiar with this procedure.
    Of the following, the BEST course of action for the foreman to take is to tell the worker

   A. that he himself must decide which procedure to follow
   B. to ask an experienced mechanic to help him with the job
   C. to go back to the old method
   D. that he does not know the answer but that he will obtain the necessary information

21. Of the following, the BEST way for a foreman to train one of his new men in a job that the man has not done before is to

   A. show the man a training film about the job
   B. let the man read in the manual about the job
   C. let the man attempt to do the entire job himself under the foreman's personal supervision
   D. assign the man to work with a more experienced man and check his work periodically

22. In setting up a work schedule for a special job, it is LEAST important for a foreman to know

   A. when the men will be available
   B. the pay rate for the men assigned
   C. the approximate time needed for the job
   D. when the needed material will be available

23. Assume that you are the foreman and that one of your men has just been injured seriously in an accident.
    Your FIRST concern should be

   A. helping the injured man
   B. finding the cause of the accident
   C. reporting the accident to your boss
   D. keeping the rest of your gang working

24. Of the following jobs, the one which a foreman should generally NOT assign to one of his men to handle is

   A. keeping material and production records
   B. putting the right man on the right job
   C. attending lectures in a safety program
   D. inspecting and maintaining tools and equipment

25. The LEAST important of the following items to include in an accident report is   25.____
    A. what action you took
    B. why you think the accident took place
    C. the time and place the accident occurred
    D. the equipment or people involved

KEY (CORRECT ANSWERS)

1. D	11. B
2. A	12. A
3. D	13. B
4. C	14. A
5. A	15. C
6. B	16. A
7. C	17. D
8. D	18. A
9. A	19. B
10. D	20. D

21. D
22. B
23. A
24. B
25. B

TEST 3

DIRECTIONS: Each question or incomplete statement is followed by several suggested answers or completions. Select the one that BEST answers the question or completes the statement. *PRINT THE LETTER OF THE CORRECT ANSWER IN THE SPACE AT THE RIGHT.*

1. Assume that you are told by another foreman that one of your men violated a safety rule. The BEST action for you, as a foreman, to take is to

    A. speak to the man about the incident
    B. tell the other foreman to leave your men alone
    C. watch this man closely in order to catch him next time
    D. give your entire gang a strong talk on safety procedures

2. Of the following, the MAIN purpose of a safety training program is to

    A. fix the blame for accidents
    B. describe accidents which have occurred
    C. maintain job progress under unsafe working conditions
    D. make the men aware of the basic causes of accidents

3. The MAIN reason for overhauling machines on a regular basis is to

    A. provide good training for the men
    B. make work for slack times
    C. minimize costly breakdowns
    D. use spare parts before they deteriorate

4. The MOST important reason for the requirement that every department operate within a budget is that a budget will

    A. enable spending to be controlled in advance
    B. clearly define the area of responsibility of a department
    C. enable a department to cut down on provisional appointments
    D. establish a good base for comparing this year's activities with last year's

5. The rules and regulations of an agency are usually LEAST useful in

    A. encouraging safe practices
    B. relieving the foremen of their supervisory responsibilities
    C. providing a fair basis for any necessary disciplinary action
    D. helping the men in the proper performance of their duties

6. The morale of employees depends to a great extent on whether they are able to influence decisions made by management on matters that directly affect the employees. On the basis of this statement, the one of the following situations which will do the MOST to raise morale is when

    A. the workers have recently received a scheduled pay raise
    B. a suggestion made by a group of workers has resulted in a change in an established procedure
    C. the supervisory staff decides to hold periodic conferences with individual workers to discuss their performance
    D. a department head makes regular visits to job sites to show his interest in each phase of the department's operations

7. Proper training encourages employees to cooperate and lowers operating costs. The statement MOST consistent with this statement is that

    A. training is only useful if costs can be lowered
    B. new workers get more benefit out of training than old employees
    C. training is a factor in improving morale and efficiency
    D. employees will refuse to cooperate if they do not receive proper training

8. The BEST of the following reasons for submitting written accident reports as soon as possible after the occurrence of an accident is that

    A. a person would tend to include too much detail after a long delay
    B. a person can more accurately recall an event which is fresh in his mind
    C. it is easier to recall events in their proper relationship after a lapse of time
    D. an experienced person can easily recall all essential detail after a long delay

9. In order for a foreman to get the work done, his orders to his men must be effective. To make sure that the orders to his men will be most effective, a foreman should

    A. tell his men the reasons why every order must be given
    B. include a great amount of detail in most orders
    C. make the orders very brief in order to keep the attention of the men
    D. give the orders and then make some checks to see if the men understand them

10. The MOST valid reason why a particular job might have a time limit set on it is that

    A. the men will be kept continuously busy
    B. this particular job is urgent
    C. maximum output can be achieved only in this way
    D. the best quality of work is thus obtained

11. If a foreman assigns an assistant foreman to supervise a group of substitute laborers temporarily, it would be MOST important for him to describe carefully to the assistant foreman the

    A. previous work experience of each substitute laborer
    B. length of time the assignment is likely to last
    C. nature and extent of the supervisory duties to be assumed
    D. reasons why substitute employees are not so dependable as regular employees

12. Suppose that your superior informs you that several of your men have complained to him about your *unusually strict supervisory methods.*
    In this situation, it would be BEST for you to

    A. ask your superior whether it is fair for him to let the men go over your head with complaints
    B. ask your superior if the men have given him any specific examples of your *strict supervisory methods*
    C. tell your superior that you are just doing your job
    D. tell your superior that you will try to ease up

13. If an experienced subordinate comes to you for a decision about a problem that he has full authority and the necessary knowledge to solve himself, it would generally be BEST for you to

    A. discuss with him the several alternative solutions to the problem and instruct him to make the decision himself
    B. make the decision but advise him that if this comes up again in the future he must make the decision himself
    C. make the decision without further comment
    D. refuse to discuss the matter and advise him that it is his responsibility to handle this himself

14. At a private conference, your superior discusses with you the failure of your section to keep up with schedules.
    He remarks that he believes you are saddled with a poor group of men and he suggests you *push them harder* to get the work done. You sincerely believe that you and your force have done the best possible job with the men and equipment available.
    In this situation, you should

    A. assume full responsibility and blame since you are the boss of the section
    B. explain the circumstances and point out why you feel that you and the men are doing a good job
    C. suggest to your superior that he himself speak to the men about the problem
    D. tactfully remind your superior that you are closer to the problem than he is

15. The number of subordinates directly reporting to a superior should not be greater than he can supervise competently.
    This is an acceptable definition of

    A. chain of command   B. span of control
    C. specialized functions   D. unity of command

16. Assume that your superior has issued orders for a change in work procedures that your men disagree with.
    As a foreman, it would be BEST for you to tell your men that

    A. nothing can be done about it at this time, even if their complaints are justified
    B. they should complain to your superior, not to you
    C. you didn't like the changes yourself and tried to talk your superior out of them
    D. you will take up their complaints with your superior

17. Suppose you are going to train your men on a new piece of equipment.
    In planning your course of instruction, to which one of the following questions should you give FIRST consideration?

    A. Exactly what do I want the men to learn in this course?
    B. How much time should I devote to this instruction?
    C. What assistance can I get in running this training program?
    D. What is the background of the men whom I will instruct?

18. You can pass the buck up but you can't pass it down. This statement implies MOST directly that a foreman

    A. is not responsible for the acts of his subordinates
    B. is responsible for the acts of his subordinates
    C. is responsible for the acts of his superiors
    D. must take the blame for anything he does wrong

19. A good foreman should know when to refer a matter to his superior and when to handle it himself.
    Of the following, the situation which a foreman would MOST appropriately refer to his superior is

    A. poor cooperation by a storekeeper in his section
    B. a complaint about poor collection service in the section
    C. a disagreement between two of his men
    D. a breakdown of recently purchased department equipment

20. If, after you have been a foreman for several years, you find that your men never complain to you about working conditions or assignments, this is MOST probably a sign that

    A. there is poor communication between you and your men
    B. the men are interested mainly in their rate of pay
    C. the men have nothing to complain about
    D. you are a very good officer

21. In hearings involving employees charged with violations, one of the main breaches of discipline is failing to obey orders.
    The CHIEF implication this should have for the foreman is that he should

    A. issue orders in writing whenever this is practicable
    B. make assignments to *teams* of men as often as possible so that the men in a team can check each other
    C. make sure his orders are understood and check on their implementation as soon as possible
    D. take disciplinary action promptly for failure to obey orders

22. Suppose that work by your men in the field is sometimes delayed because they wait for you to arrive to make certain decisions before continuing with their work.
    As a foreman, this should indicate to you the need for

    A. breaking up job assignments into smaller units
    B. developing more initiative in your men
    C. having the men select someone to be in charge if you are not there
    D. issuing complete instructions if you know you are going to be away

23. Before you turn in a report you have written of an investigation that you have made, you discover some additional information you didn't know about before.
Whether or not you rewrite your report to include this additional information should depend MAINLY on the

    A. amount of time remaining before the report is due
    B. established policy of the department covering the subject matter of the report
    C. bearing this information will have on the conclusions of the report
    D. number of people who will eventually review the report

24. When a foreman submits a periodic report to the district office, he should realize that the CHIEF importance of such a report is that it

    A. is the principal method of checking on the efficiency of the officer and his subordinates
    B. is something to which frequent reference will be made
    C. eliminates the need for any personal follow-up or inspection by higher echelons
    D. permits the agency head to exercise his functions of direction, supervision, and control better

25. Conclusions and recommendations are usually better placed at the end rather than at the beginning of a report because

    A. the person preparing the report may decide to change some of the conclusions and recommendations before he reaches the end of the report
    B. they are the most important part of the report
    C. they can be judged better by the person to whom the report is sent after he reads the facts and investigations which come earlier in the report
    D. they can be referred to quickly when needed without reading the rest of the report

KEY (CORRECT ANSWERS)

1. A
2. D
3. C
4. A
5. B

6. B
7. C
8. B
9. D
10. B

11. C
12. B
13. A
14. B
15. B

16. D
17. A
18. B
19. D
20. A

21. C
22. B
23. C
24. D
25. C

EXAMINATION SECTION
TEST 1

DIRECTIONS: Each question or incomplete statement is followed by several suggested answers or completions. Select the one that BEST answers the question or completes the statement. *PRINT THE LETTER OF THE CORRECT ANSWER IN THE SPACE AT THE RIGHT.*

1. Which one of the following statements pertaining to on-the-job training is *most usually* considered CORRECT?

    A. The foreman will get better results by praising a mechanic for a good job than criticizing him for a bad one.
    B. A mechanic who learns slowly will automatically retain more of what he learns than will a person who learns fast.
    C. An older mechanic learns more easily than does a younger person.
    D. It is best to learn the hardest part of a job first and then go on to the easier parts.

1.____

2. Of the following statements, the one which will be MOST effective in helping a foreman develop cooperation, interest, and enthusiasm among his men in performing their work is if he

    A. maintains close personal contact with his men
    B. makes work assignments in exactly the same way
    C. *covers up* when any of his men makes a serious error
    D. realizes that it is his men who will get the job done

2.____

3. Generally, the MAIN reason for a foreman to investigate accidents is to

    A. help prevent a recurrence of the accident
    B. help determine if replacement parts are needed
    C. provide information for a possible lawsuit
    D. prevent false compensation claims

3.____

4. Assume that you are having a discussion with one of your mechanics about his job performance. During the discussion, you make an unfavorable comment in between two complimentary comments.
For you to do this is a

    A. *good idea* because this makes it easier for the mechanic to be criticized
    B. *bad idea* because criticism should not be softened with any kind words
    C. *good idea* because more of your unfavorable comments will be remembered this way
    D. *bad idea* because a mechanic deserves to hear the straight truth

4.____

5. Of the following, at a face-to-face discussion with a mechanic about his job duties and responsibilities, it is MOST desirable to

    A. give the mechanic just enough knowledge to work until the next such discussion
    B. let the mechanic have a good understanding of how he is doing on the job
    C. deal with some of the mechanic's complaints but not all of them at one time
    D. remain aloof from the mechanic so the mechanic does not ask further questions

5.____

6. A foreman conducts periodic meetings for his own group of mechanics. The topics MOST often discussed at these group meetings would PROBABLY be

   A. efficiency reports, worker evaluations, and promotion opportunities
   B. disciplinary actions, grievances, and suspensions
   C. incentive awards, tenants' complaints, and employee suggestions
   D. work schedules, work procedures, and safety

7. Suppose your supervisor has asked you to prepare a written report on the morale problems of your work force. The one of the following observations about report writing that is MOST important for you to remember is to

   A. use the most difficult vocabulary you can
   B. make the report as long as possible
   C. use language appropriate for the people reading the report
   D. try to liven up your report so people will find it interesting

8. When a foreman writes a report, it is MOST important to prepare an outline because the outline

   A. will impress his supervisor
   B. will indicate areas to study more fully
   C. can serve as a handy summary at the end of the report
   D. will help him organize the material for his report

9. A newly assigned mechanic fails to carry out an assignment and claims that he did not understand the orders.
   Of the following, the BEST way to handle the situation is to

   A. take his word for it and see if it happens again
   B. have the incident noted in the employee's record and tell the employee afterwards
   C. give the assignment to another more experienced mechanic
   D. take formal disciplinary action against the mechanic to make sure that it does not happen again

10. Your supervisor makes a habit of bypassing you in issuing orders to your mechanics. Of the following courses of action, the BEST one for you to take in this situation is to

    A. tell your employees that they are to take orders only from you
    B. have your employees comply with the orders and have them report back directly to your supervisor
    C. talk to your supervisor and point out that the practice can be harmful to efficiency and morale
    D. tell your supervisor that he is not to give orders to your employees except in emergencies

11. You find that one of your better mechanics has become slipshod in making preventive maintenance inspections. Of the following, the BEST way to handle this situation is to

    A. warn him that if his work does not improve, you will have him transferred to another crew
    B. issue a general notice to all mechanics on the need of making thorough inspections
    C. tell the mechanic that he can no longer be relied on to make good inspections
    D. call in the mechanic and suggest ways in which he can improve his inspections

12. A necessary maintenance job has to be rotated among your men because it is a repetitious, boring type of job. Through an oversight, you assign this same job twice in a row to one of your men. When the man complains, you realize that you should have assigned the job to another man.
Of the following statements, the one which is the BEST way to handle the situation is to tell the man that you

    A. will decide which assignments he will get
    B. made a mistake and that you will try to correct the situation
    C. gave him the job because you felt that he was the best man for it
    D. gave him the job because it was an emergency situation

12.____

13. Some foremen make it a practice to always find a fault in the work done by their mechanics, no matter how good a job the men do.
For a foreman to do this is a

    A. *good idea* because it keeps the mechanics from feeling too confident
    B. *bad idea* because it is best for the foreman to point to major faults instead of minor ones
    C. *good idea* because it will encourage the mechanics to try harder
    D. *bad idea* because the mechanics will lose their feelings of achievement

13.____

14. A mechanic comes to you with a complaint which upon investigation clearly is of an imaginary nature.
The BEST reason for giving his complaint serious attention is that, if the matter is not resolved, the mechanic

    A. will complain about it until someone listens
    B. will start taking time off from work
    C. can stir up the rest of the workers
    D. may go to the union about the matter

14.____

15. You are considering asking one of your mechanics for advice on a certain work project. For a foreman to ask advice from a subordinate would be MOST properly considered as a(n)

    A. way to get more production from the mechanic
    B. means of learning new work techniques from the mechanic
    C. compliment to the mechanic, as long as the foreman is sincere
    D. idea to keep the mechanic *on his toes* all the time

15.____

16. You assign a job to one of your experienced mechanics.
You notice that he does the job in a way which is different from the way you do it.
The BEST practice for you to follow in this case is to

    A. stop him and tell him how you want the job done
    B. let him do it his way and evaluate the results
    C. immediately take the mechanic off the job without an explanation
    D. wait until the job is done and then tell him that he should not change the existing methods

16.____

17. One of your mechanics comes to you and asks you for advice about a serious emotional problem he cannot handle. Which one of the following would be the BEST approach for you to take in handling this matter?

    A. Immediately tell him to stop worrying and that everything will work out.
    B. Advise him yourself based on your own experience.
    C. Listen attentively and tactfully suggest he seek professional help.
    D. Tell him that since it is his problem, he will have to find his own solution.

17.____

18. The one of the following which would indicate that a foreman's work attitude is WRONG is that he

    A. occasionally gets angry in front of his mechanics
    B. looks for good traits in his mechanics
    C. does not get too upset about his mechanics' mistakes
    D. always complains about his work

18.____

19. Of the following procedures, the one that would be LEAST effective in improving the job performance of subordinates is to

    A. have them evaluate their own performance so that they can determine how well they work
    B. help them set specific goals that are within their capabilities
    C. encourage them by commenting on a positive factor in their performance
    D. ask them directly about their personal affairs to determine if factors not related to the job are influencing their job performance

19.____

20. The one of the following instances in which it is BEST for a foreman to give a *spoken* order to his men is when

    A. many people are responsible for the job
    B. the job is a simple and routine one
    C. a mistake would have serious results
    D. many levels of supervision are involved

20.____

21. One of your mechanics, on his own initiative, is doing much more work than the other men. The man is well-liked, and all the other mechanics are doing an acceptable amount of work.
    Of the following, the BEST course of action for you to take in this case is to

    A. publicly praise the man as a model for the others
    B. tell the man in private that he should not do more work than the others
    C. allow the situation to continue unchanged
    D. criticize the others for failing to meet the standard set by the man

21.____

22. The one of the following instances in which it is BEST to give a *written* order to your men is when the

    A. job is a repetitive one
    B. job is a short one
    C. job involves many new details
    D. progress of the job can be easily checked

22.____

23. The MOST likely result that will occur if a foreman constantly *jumps to conclusions* is that he will   23.____

    A. lose the respect of his mechanics and superiors
    B. be correct in his conclusions half of the time
    C. inspire respect from his men
    D. gradually learn to make important decisions quickly

24. The one of the following statements on supervision that is MOST *likely* to be CORRECT is: 24.____

    A. Production is greatest when the foreman constantly criticizes his mechanics
    B. The foreman who consistently checks the work habits of his mechanics is able to correct many problems promptly
    C. The best way for a foreman to control his men is to give discipline for discipline's sake
    D. Occasional supervision of the work force is all that is necessary for your mechanics to work more efficiently

25. The one of the following that is the LEAST important reason for you to delegate work to a mechanic under your supervision is that   25.____

    A. the mechanic will have to learn to do the work
    B. it is a means of motivation
    C. your work load will be reduced
    D. it will reduce the mechanic's work responsibilities

KEY (CORRECT ANSWERS)

1. A		11. D	
2. D		12. B	
3. A		13. D	
4. A		14. C	
5. B		15. C	
6. D		16. B	
7. C		17. C	
8. D		18. D	
9. A		19. D	
10. C		20. B	

21. C
22. C
23. A
24. B
25. D

TEST 2

DIRECTIONS: Each question or incomplete statement is followed by several suggested answers or completions. Select the one that BEST answers the question or completes the statement. *PRINT THE LETTER OF THE CORRECT ANSWER IN THE SPACE AT THE RIGHT.*

1. The one of the following that is the LEAST important characteristic of a good foreman is 1.____

    A. a great deal of formal schooling
    B. sensitivity to the problems of others
    C. ability in working with people
    D. the ability to communicate with his men

2. Assume it is necessary to criticize a mechanic's attitude toward his work habits. 2.____
   Of the following, the BEST practice to follow would be to focus on

    A. the mechanic's character instead of his behavior
    B. comments you have heard about the man, rather than what you have observed
    C. general principles of how the mechanic should do his job instead of a specific incident
    D. sharing ideas and information with the mechanic rather than just giving advice

3. Of the following, the BEST method for a foreman to use when reprimanding a mechanic is to 3.____

    A. prepare a report reprimanding the mechanic and give it to him to avoid an argument
    B. reprimand the mechanic at a group meeting
    C. reprimand the mechanic in private, where no other mechanics are present
    D. ask your supervisor to reprimand the mechanic in your presence

4. Assume that upon assigning one of your mechanics to a certain job, he makes an unfavorable comment to you about the assignment. 4.____
   The one of the following possible approaches that would be BEST for you to take in this instance is for you to tell the man

    A. to do as he is told at all times
    B. that you will consider his opinion when you make further assignments
    C. to write down his comment and submit it to the suggestion program
    D. that he is probably right but that your supervisor is responsible for the assignment

5. One of your mechanics has just come back to work from sick leave and is working at a little less than peak efficiency. You decide not to say anything to the man because you once had the same illness yourself. 5.____
   For you to put yourself in another person's place is a

    A. *good idea* because a foreman should be sensitive to the feelings of his workers
    B. *bad idea* because a foreman should not give his men reason to think he is soft-hearted
    C. *good* idea because if the foreman does a favor for the mechanic, the mechanic will do a favor for the foreman
    D. *bad idea* because a foreman should expect uniform production from his men at all times

6. It would be POOR practice for a foreman to

   A. personally instruct a mechanic in a difficult maintenance procedure
   B. learn the relative abilities of his men by observing the quality of their work
   C. explain to his supervisor why work output decreased during a certain week
   D. complain about the quality of a mechanic's work to the man's co-workers

7. Of the following, the situation which would MOST severely test a foreman's supervisory skill would be

   A. the assignment of a regular job which must be expedited
   B. the absorption into the group under his supervision of a number of mechanics newly transferred to the shop
   C. the assignment to replace a foreman who has retired
   D. attempting to improve good housekeeping on the job

8. A mechanic repeatedly performs an important maintenance procedure incorrectly. In this situation, it would be MOST correct to conclude that the

   A. procedure is probably too difficult for the average mechanic
   B. written instructions for this job are incorrect
   C. foreman is exercising poor supervision
   D. mechanic has personal problems

9. If a foreman has a mechanic in his gang who is constantly passing the buck to his co-workers when jobs he has worked on turn out to be unsatisfactory, then it would be BEST for the foreman to

   A. complain about this man to the supervisor
   B. reassign him to work with different individuals
   C. give him work assignments which will fix responsibility on him
   D. let the co-workers who have been blamed deal with him in their own way

10. Of the following, the characteristic which will do the MOST to assure a foreman of the respect of his subordinates is the foreman's ability to

    A. maintain good relations with his supervisor
    B. plan work assignments in advance
    C. maintain rigid discipline
    D. technically assist his men in their work assignments

11. You notice that a mechanic in your gang wears rubber-soled shoes. As his foreman, you should

    A. *commend* him because these shoes insure safety from electrical shock
    B. *commend* him because these shoes produce less fatigue
    C. *disapprove* because these shoes are slippery and easily pierced
    D. *disapprove* because these shoes rot quickly when in contact with grease and oil

12. You are asked by your supervisor to have your men use a newly designed tester. Of the following, the information your supervisor would be MOST interested in obtaining from you would be

    A. an estimate of the durability of the new tester
    B. whether better production can be secured with the new tester
    C. the space requirements for the new tester
    D. the power requirements for the new tester

13. An *impartial* foreman is one who is

    A. sincere   B. watchful   C. industrious   D. fair

14. To be MOST effective, a report should be

    A. simple and concise
    B. long and impressive
    C. written with perfect grammar and punctuation
    D. typed instead of written

15. If one of your mechanics comes to work obviously drunk, the BEST thing to do is to

    A. give the man an easy job where he can't hurt himself
    B. let the man *sleep it off* in the morning and put him to work when the effects have apparently worn off
    C. send the man home
    D. give the man a hard job where he can *sweat it out*

16. Keeping tools in good condition does NOT

    A. cut costs
    B. make work easier
    C. lessen the possibility of accidents
    D. reduce the supervision required

17. In the use of hand tools, injuries are LEAST likely to happen when working

    A. carefully
    B. with poorly conditioned and dull tools
    C. while day-dreaming
    D. with the wrong tool for the job

18. One of your mechanics offers a suggestion to improve the method of doing a job. The BEST thing to do is to tell the man that

    A. the job has always been done the same way and, therefore, it must be the best way
    B. you will check his suggestion to see whether it really is a better way of doing the job
    C. he should make the suggestion to the chief engineer
    D. he should discuss it with two other mechanics and, if they agree with him, you will try the suggested method

19. One of the mechanics in your gang complains that the other men in the gang are *riding* him.
    The FIRST action you should take is to

    A. transfer the man to another gang
    B. report the matter to your superior
    C. investigate to see if the complaint is true
    D. bring the other men in the gang up on charges

20. One of the mechanics in your gang complains about having to do a hard job.
    The BEST thing for you to do is to

    A. ignore him
    B. explain to him that all men must do their fair share of the hard jobs
    C. tell him that his next job will be an easy one
    D. take him off this job

21. The BEST foreman is *usually* the

    A. *best* mechanic
    B. *fastest* worker
    C. man in service the *longest*
    D. *ablest* leader

22. Men will respect their foreman MOST if he

    A. acts sternly with them
    B. does not show favoritism
    C. is quick to criticize their errors
    D. does not enforce all the rules and regulations

23. A newly appointed mechanic has been assigned to your gang.
    Of the following, the BEST practice to follow with this man is to

    A. immediately put him to work with the gang since his work requires no special skill
    B. allow him to do only the type of work he says he is capable of doing until he can learn the other jobs
    C. instruct the man as to how the job should be done before putting him to work
    D. give the man the most difficult job since the best method of learning is by doing

24. Of the following, the statement that is CORRECT is:

    A. Every worker can do the same amount of work
    B. The man with the most seniority will work the fastest
    C. The strongest man will do the most work
    D. The amount of york a man does can be increased by improving morale

25. Preventive maintenance cannot be effective unless there is (are)

    A. an efficient repair shop
    B. adequate replacement tools and equipment
    C. instructions to use care in the handling of tools and equipment
    D. regular periodic inspections of tools and equipment

KEY (CORRECT ANSWERS)

1. A
2. D
3. C
4. B
5. A

6. D
7. B
8. C
9. C
10. B

11. C
12. B
13. D
14. A
15. C

16. D
17. A
18. B
19. C
20. B

21. D
22. B
23. C
24. D
25. D

THE FOREMAN
BASIC FUNDAMENTALS OF SUPERVISION AND MANAGEMENT

CONTENTS

	Page
I. THE JOB OF THE FOREMAN	1
His Duties and Responsibilities	1
Human Relations Duties	1
Training Duties	1
Production Duties	1
1. Schedules	1
2. Quality	2
3. Costs	2
4. General Production Duties	2
His Authority	2
1. Supervision	2
2. Use of Productive Facilities	2
3. Maintenance of Quality	2
4. Control of jobs	2
Special Problems of the Foreman in a Small Plant	3
II. BASIC RESPONSIBILITIES	3
Getting Production Out on Time	3
1. Materials	4
2. Schedule Balance	4
3. Work Simplification	4
4. Machine Utilization	4
5. Worker Utilization	4
Maintaining Quality Standards	5
Holding Production Costs Down	5
1. Direct Labor Costs	7
2. Indirect Labor Costs	7
3. Material Utilization	8
4. Machine Utilization	8
5. Methods Improvement	8
How Top Management Can Help Foremen Improve Efficiency	9
III. THE FOREMAN'S TRAINING FUNCTION	9
Training New Employees	9
1. Explaining Company Policies	10
2. Instruction Covering Shop Operations	10
3. Coaching Covering the Job of a New Employee	10

	Training Employees Promoted to New Jobs	10
	Training an Understudy	10
	Other Training Responsibilities	11
	1. Orientation of Salesmen and Other Company Personnel	11
	2. Special Training Sessions for Employees	11
IV.	**THE FOREMAN'S PERSONAL RELATIONSHIPS AND CONTACTS**	11
	Relationships With Workers	11
	Contacts With Supervisors in Other Departments	12
	Relationships With Superiors	12
	Contacts With Unions and Union Officials	12
	Contacts With the Public	13
V.	**DEVELOPING BETTER FOREMEN**	13
	Qualifications Which Foremen Need	13
	1. Leadership Ability	14
	2. Organizing Ability	14
	3. Character	14
	4. Judgment	14
	5. Technical Skill and Mechanical Skill	14
	6. Education	14
	7. Initiative	15
	8. Human Interest	15
	9. Physical and Mental Requirements	15
	Finding Prospects	15
	What Kind of Training	15
	Solving the Problem in Small Plants	16
	1. Cooperation With Other Small Plants	16
	2. Cooperation With Colleges and Universities	16
	3. Use of Programs Developed By Larger Companies	16
	4. Use of Supervisory Programs Developed by Management Associations	17
	Measuring the Results	17
	How Top Management Promotes Foreman Development	18
	1. Incentive Payments	18
	2. Authority	18
	3. Prestige	18

CONCISE TEXT
THE FOREMAN
BASIC FUNDAMENTALS OF SUPERVISION AND MANAGEMENT

I. THE JOB OF THE FOREMAN

- **His duties and responsibilities**
- **His authority**
- **Special problems of the foreman in a small plant**

A foreman is the member of plant management who has been delegated the authority to manage a shop, a function, or a department. He is the one whom the folks in the shop call boss; he is the one they look to for instructions and supervision; and he shoulders the responsibility for all work done by those who report to him. In short, he is the first line of management. In this position he is a key figure both as a production manager and in the plant's relationships with its employees.

His Duties and Responsibilities

The foreman's job is to use the men, machines, and material assigned to him for the purpose of getting out production under conditions specified by his superiors. In order to accomplish this objective, he has to perform a multitude of duties and responsibilities.

Human Relations Duties

1. To maintain good relationships with employees, with other departments in the plant, with his superiors, with customers, with unions, and with the public.
2. To settle grievances—one of his most important duties.
3. To be familiar with the union contract if there is one, and to run the shop in strict accordance with it.
4. To be familiar with company policies and interpret them to the workers as management has explained them to him
5. To exercise leadership and supervision over the people assigned to him.
6. To develop and maintain job interest among his employees.
7. To be available when those who report to him need help or assistance, whether it be of a business or personal nature.

Training Duties

1. To inform new employees assigned to him about company policies.
2. To see that new employees receive adequate job instruction.
3. To train an understudy who can take his place in the event he is absent, or is promoted, or resigns.

Production Duties:

1. Schedules: He is expected to get the production out in accordance with schedules prescribed by his superiors; to coordinate the various activities in his department for

---

*n.b. Pronouns are used collectively

the purpose of eliminating delays and bottlenecks; and to see that the men, materials, and machines assigned to him are fully utilized.
2. Quality: He is expected to protect the customer from the receipt of faulty products through proper shop precautions.
3. Costs: He is expected to keep production costs within the budget approved by his superiors
4. General Production Duties: He is expected to be constantly alert to new methods and procedures which will improve quality, reduce delays, and reduce production costs; he is also expected to see that all production activities conform with plant safety regulations.

Although the duties of a foreman vary by necessity from plant to plant, the ones listed above cover the basic responsibilities which most foreman are expected to shoulder.

His Authority

A foreman's authority to make decisions and take action is delegated to him by his superiors. While this, too, must of necessity vary according to the circumstances, most foreman have the following general types of authority.

1. Supervision: This involves the authority to exercise full supervision over the men, materials, machines, and supplies assigned to his department—within the limits of company policies.
2. Use of Productive Facilities: This involves the authority to requisition materials, supplies, and personnel and incur certain other expenses within the limits of his approved budget.
3. Maintenance of Quality: This involves the authority to reject any item produced in his shop which falls in his opinion to meet standards of quality as prescribed by his superiors.
4. Control of Jobs: This involves, for some foremen, the authority to hire and fire.

A foreman's influence is often greater than his specific authority. In certain areas, his superior may regard him as a personal representative, and by virtue of that fact, the foreman's recommendations carry considerable weight. For example, his recommendations concerning personnel, product design, the need for more shop space, new production processes or formulas, and new equipment are given careful consideration. He is usually closer to problems of this nature than any other official in the plant. In the eyes of the workers, the foreman's authority within the shop is all inclusive. If by chance the workers have any question on this score, it is only because the foreman's superiors fail to back him up adequately.

In exercising his authority, and in accepting responsibilities, the foreman acts as a member of a team, the management team. But as in any kind of team work, he must also rely upon his superiors for advice, guidance, and information. Likewise, his superiors are dependent on him for information and suggestions. Crystallizing this concept of teamwork in the minds of all members of management is perhaps the greatest single element of help that can be given to foremen. It encourages greater cooperation between the foreman's shop and other departments, and as a result, the whole company benefits from it. In addition, the foreman needs the cooperation and support of every department with which he comes in contact if he is to do his job effectively.

Special Problems of the Foreman in a Small Plant

The problems of a foreman in a small plant are often different from those of a foreman in a large company. There are two basic reasons why this is true.

First, small plants can't always afford the services of those specialized departments which are accepted as an essential part of the organization in a large plant. For example, relatively few small plants enjoy the benefit of time-study specialists, of full-time production inspectors, or of separate machine maintenance departments. Although such services may not be handled by specialized personnel, the work still has to be done, and quite often the responsibility for doing it is assigned to the foreman. As a result, the duties and problems of small-plant foremen are usually broader in scope than are those of foremen in a larger plant.

Second, a small plant typically operates on a more intimate basis than a large one. Thus, the relationships between department heads are more personal, and as a result everybody gets to know everybody else much better than is possible in a larger plant. Similarly, department heads are more dependent upon each other for cooperation and help. In such a situation, the foreman has to be doubly alert to the value of good personal relationships, because one unfortunate experience with just one department head in the plant can create a problem between himself and the heads of several other departments. If such an incident occurs, and it results in less cooperation between his shop and other departments, his value to the company is greatly diminished. For this reason the foreman must be an accepted member of the small plant family, in fact as well as theory, or else he has no place in the organization. Therefore, the smaller the plant, the more important personal relationships become.

II. BASIC RESPONSIBILITIES OF A FOREMAN

The foreman has three basic responsibilities: Getting production out on time, getting production to conform with quality standards, and getting production out at the least possible cost.

Unless a foreman can satisfy these three responsibilities, he is unable to live up to the requirements of his job.

Getting Production Out on Time

The foreman's department has to satisfy certain production quotas because customers want to receive their purchases within a certain period of time. In order to make sure that customers get their shipments within the time specified, one of the foreman's superiors usually develops a production schedule in consultation with the foreman, the sales department, and other interested departments. This schedule then becomes a timetable to which operations must be gear. It places a maximum limit on the amount of time that can be allowed to produce a given number of units. The foreman's objective, insofar as schedules are concerned, should not only be to get production out on schedule, but to get it put as much ahead of schedule as possible, within the resources of his department.

In meeting schedule deadlines, a foreman needs to maintain a set of figures which will tell him at the end of each day how his shop is producing. These figures should tell him that the shop is either adequately or inadequately organized for getting the work out on time. Without such information, his ability to meet schedules is left up to chance.

For example, if a schedule calls for the production of 220 units in a 30-day month, the foreman knows that his shop has 22 work days in which to do the job required. When, during any given day, less than 10 units are produced, he knows he is falling behind schedule and can take remedial action before the production deadline arrives. The foreman's superiors are also interested in these figures and he has a responsibility to keep them posted at all times as to the progress in relation to the scheduled requirement.

Sometimes production falls behind schedule for reasons which have to be referred to higher authority for correction. For example, shipments of raw materials which are needed to produce the finished product may be delayed by the supplier; abnormal sickness may require overtime by others and approval to thus add to expenses; or a machine breaks down and delay production to such an extent that the schedule has to be revised.

However, most of the reasons for a shop falling behind schedule are due to internal conditions. Ingenuity of the foreman in identifying the causes and taking remedial action is a test of his ability to hold down the job of foreman. Some of the most common conditions which lie within the authority of the foreman to correct are as follows:

1. Materials: The material which goes into the production process may be located in an inconvenient spot. It may be placed where it is so inaccessible or located so far away from the workers that must valuable production time is lost in transporting the material to the machines. Frequently, a more efficient arrangement of materials will solve the production lag problem. The foreman has to be alert to the need for having raw materials placed in the best location.

2. Schedule Balance: Oftentimes the workers engaged in producing a certain part of the product will get ahead of those who are producing other parts. This leaves workers who turn out the finished items standing idle until the parts from the lagging operations shop are available. Since all parts of a given product must be produced on schedule, if the deadline for completed units is to be met, the foreman often has to redistribute the number of men and machines assigned to a given phase of the operation in order to maintain the proper balance of output between the various operations being performed.

3. Work Simplification: Sometimes the number of operations performed by each worker are so great or so unrelated that the rate of production is slowed down. In such a case production can be speeded up if the job of each worker is broken down so that he has a smaller variety of steps to perform. Frequently, depending upon the nature of the produce being produced, this saves time because it reduces the motions of changing from one operation to another. This is a possibility the foreman has to consider, for often it is the key to quicker production.

4. Machine Utilization: Scheduling the work in proper sequence and with balanced timing is essential if the foreman expects to get maximum use out of each available machine. Regular inspection and maintenance of each machine is also essential if disruptive breakdowns are to be avoided. Down time is expensive. It adds to production costs, to say nothing of the cost of the investment in equipment.

5. Worker Utilization: Placing workers on those phases of the operation where they can do most effective work is also an aid to meeting production schedules. The foreman has to know how much work each employee is producing, and how his production compares with those around him in order that the slow ones may be singled out for consultation. A worker who is a laggard on one job may do better work on other jobs for which he is better adapted.

In order to meet production requirement, a foreman must maintain a delicate balance between men, the machines, and the materials in his shop. Failure to maintain the balance will result in disrupted production and eventual failure to meet the scheduled deadline.

Maintaining Quality Standards

Production has to conform with quality standards as prescribed by top management because the customer will return any unit which fails to meet those standards. If such returns reach significant proportions, the reputation and prestige of the plant suffers. Because of the embarrassment arising from the sale of faulty good to customers, most plants have an arrangement whereby finished goods are inspected before they are shipped to the customer. If, upon inspection, it is found that the product meets all quality standards, it is approved for shipment. If it doesn't, it is rejected and sent back to the shop for more attention. The practice of conducting such inspections is commonly referred to as "quality control." Some plants, especially those which produce critical items (such as parachutes), inspect every unit before it is "o.k.'d." But this is expensive, and hence other plants use a type of statistical quality control. This is a system whereby only one unit out of a given number of units is checked, with the assumption that if the units checked are found all right, then those in between are likewise all right. The system is becoming more popular in plants and is proving to be effective.

The ideal arrangement is to have finished production inspected by someone who reports to the foreman's superior. This is desirable because the inspector is checking work which the foreman is responsible for producing, and a person who has no responsibility to the foreman, or who has had no part in the production of the items can usually be more objective in his inspections. However, in some of the smaller plant, when inspectors are not carried on the payroll, the inspection function may be delegated to the foreman himself.

Under either arrangement, the foreman should maintain the following information concerning units which are rejected, for use in improving the quality of production.

1. The number of units rejected within the plant each day, week, or month (whichever is most practicable.).
2. The number of units rejected by customers each day, week, or month.
3. The name of the worker who produced the unit, if such information is available.

The inspector should keep both the foreman and his superiors advised of the number of units rejected by him. The foreman's superiors should keep the foreman and the inspector advised regarding the number of units rejected by the customers. These records should be used by all three parties to determine whether the number of rejections is excessive. If the number of units rejected exceeds the average rate, it is then up to the foreman to check with the employees responsible and reanalyze his procedures to determine what corrective action is necessary. However, even though the number of rejections is below normal, the foreman still has a responsibility to devise ways and means of effecting further reductions. The best foremen have the lowest rejection rates.

Holding Production Costs Down

The use of shop budgets for cost control purposes is the most effective means for making the foreman cost conscious. This is true because he knows that he either has to live within his budget or explain the reasons why. In many plants, the cost accountant prepares a monthly report showing detailed types of expenses as charged to each department in relation to the amount budgeted. This report is useful to top management because it tells how effectively the foreman has controlled his expenses during the previous month. It also serves as a useful supervisory tool for the foreman because it tells him what particular expenditure exceeded the budget, which enables him to know in which area remedial action is necessary.

However, if the foreman is to operate his department as effectively as possible, he can't wait until the end of the month to see how good its performance has been. He usually needs to know on the following day how well he did the day before; in other words, he needs daily expense figures which he can compare with daily budget figures. Such figures on a rounded basis can be easily developed by the foreman himself. All he needs to do is take the previous month's budget report and develop from it average daily budget figures which will give him a fairly good idea of what his maximum daily expenses for the current month should be. He can then develop an estimate on the following day which will tell him what his approximate costs were on the previous day. By comparing the previous day's estimate with his estimated daily expense budget he can get a fairly good idea of how well his expenses are being controlled. If accurate daily performance records can be developed, they of course are more desirable than estimated figures. But many small plants do not have the resources for keeping detailed expense records on a daily basis.

The budget covering the foreman's shop should be prepared by the foreman himself. This not only accentuates the importance of the foreman's responsibility, but it is a more realistic way of preparing a budget. The foreman is closer to the needs of his department than anyone else and if the budget is prepared by someone farther removed from the shop activities, it cannot be all-inclusive and will usually result in the foreman asking for authority to exceed the budget because something was overlooked when it was originally set up. If, after the foreman prepares the budget, his superiors want to cut some of the estimated costs, they then have a more realistic set of figures from which they can estimate what adjustments should be made.

Once a foreman's budget has been established, he should clearly understand that he is expected to keep his expenditures within budgetary limitations. Authority to exceed the budgeted amount should be granted only upon the specific request of the foreman, and only after it has been determined how far he should exceed the budget and for what type of expenditure.

A good foreman not only wants to keep within his budget, he wants to keep his expenditures as far below the budget as possible because he wants to be a good enough administrator to get the production out with the least possible cost.

A budget report to be effectively used as a means of controlling expenditures in the shop should be issued in final form by the accounting people once a month. It should show both the actual and budgeted monthly expense for the following items:

1. Direct labor costs
2. Indirect labor costs
3. Material cost
4. Maintenance costs
5. Costs of supplies, including tools
6. Light, heat, power, and telephone cost

These are controllable costs (some, of course, are more controllable than others) which the foreman should be conscious of at all times. Other items of a non-controllable nature are also usually included in the budget report. However, as long as the foreman gets reports covering his controllable expenses, he has something which he can use to guide him in his efforts to run a more efficient shop.

The foreman has to be continually conscious of the cost which results from everything that goes on in the shop. Here is a list of some of the major areas on which a foreman has to keep a particularly watchful eye if he is to successfully hold expenses down:

1. Direct Labor Costs: You don't normally cut costs by cuffing wages because lower wages attract less efficient people and in the long run, a wage cut increases labor costs. In fact, some shops have been known to cut costs by raising wages, because through higher wages they were able to attract more efficient people. As a result, fewer people were needed to turn out the production. The real personnel costs that can and must be controlled are those resulting from absenteeism, turnover, accidents, and improper utilization of workers.

    A worker who is guilty of excessive absenteeism increases shop costs because the work schedule of the shop has to be readjusted each time he is absent. That costs money. This is a matter which should be ironed out on a personal basis between the employee and the foreman on the merits of each case.

    Excessive turnover is also costly. It is costly in terms of the time and effort used (a) to find and process replacements; (b) to train new employees to your equipment and your methods. Furthermore, it is costly in terms of productivity; it is usually several weeks or longer before the performance of new employees equals that of your experienced workers. The problem of excessive turnover can, in many cases, be clarified by getting from each employee the reasons for his leaving. Both the foreman and the personnel department should be interested in such information. Once the true reasons for turnover are known, corrective action can be taken. High turnover is frequently caused by poor selection, low wages, or poor supervision on the part of the foreman.

    When a worker is incapacitated because of an occupational accident, not only does the company temporarily lose his services, but hospital bills, increased workmen's compensation assessments, increased insurance rates, and law suit are apt to result. While not all of these charges would be reflected in the foreman's budget, nevertheless hospital charge and other miscellaneous items become a part of his labor costs.

    Failure by the foreman to utilize fully the time an employee is on the job results in increased production costs not only because the worker is being paid for time he has not worked, but because failure to use the regular man-hours available may force the foreman to resort to overtime work in order to get production out on time. A foreman should organize the next day's work before he leaves the shop at night. This is the best way to assure full utilization of all employees.

2. Indirect Labor Costs: These are the labor costs which have nothing to do with actual manufacturing or production costs, such as the cost of labor required sweeping the floors, and repairing the machines. In order to keep indirect labor costs to a minimum, the foreman will do well to keep his eye on two major items: the cost of maintaining machines and the cost of handling raw materials. In small plants especially, responsibility for the costs of these functions falls upon the production foreman.

    Experience proves that it is cheaper to inspect machines at regular intervals and replace worn parts than to wait until they break down. For when a machine breaks down, its repair usually costs more than keeping the machine in good condition through the process of regular inspection. In addition, a broken-down machine disrupts production, which results in even greater expense.

Perhaps one of the most overlooked expense items in the indirect labor category is the cost of materials handling. It has been estimated, for example, that 36 percent of the labor dollar in the electrical industry is spent in moving materials destined to go into the production process from one place to another. When the material arrives at the plant, it is moved into the warehouse. While there it may be moved several times to make room for other incoming shipments. Then it is moved to the shop, where it may be moved again several times before it is finally used in production. Such a procedure not only make indirect labor costs excessively high, but also increases the cost of material because the more the material is moved, the more it is in danger of being damaged.

3. Material Utilization: The foreman can cut the cost of materials by developing standardized procedures for employees to follow in cutting up a piece of material. Most pieces come in standard sizes and lend themselves to formal cutting procedures which can result in considerable savings. A furniture factory, for instance, has found that a piece of plywood which comes in standard 4x8 foot sizes can make a small bookcase with only one-half of a board foot to spare, if the cutting is done in a certain way. If the piece is cut any other way, it takes two such pieces, with a lot of material left over. Most of it cannot be used at all, and the part that is usable can be used only by disrupting the assembly line. Material costs are a big factor in production and proper utilization can help hold production costs down.

4. Machine Utilization: Machines cost money whether they are utilized or not because they depreciate and become obsolete. To justify these costs, machines should be fully utilized at all times through proper work organization. Therefore, before the foreman goes home at night, he should know exactly how every employee and machine will be utilized when the shop opens up the next day.

5. Methods Improvement: To do his job of keeping costs down to a minimum, a foreman must be, in addition to everything else, an "efficiency expert." He must constantly be on the lookout for better, cheaper, and easier ways of getting the production out. He should consider such things as the number of steps a worker must take in going from one operation to another; a rearrangement of equipment will save money if that will cut down on the number of steps required. He needs to consider the number of motions a worker must go through to complete a given operation; if a change in procedure will make some motions unnecessary, he has saved the company money.

In attempting to make his shop as efficient as possible, the foreman can make progress if he will look to his employees for ideas. They are in a position to see many things which he is either unable or too busy to see. Some of the best ideas for increasing efficiency in plants come from employee. A formalized suggestion plan promoted by the foremen will serve as a stimulus for employees to develop new ideas and turn them in. A suggestion plan if properly promoted can be one of the most effective steps toward greater plant efficiency.

How Top Management Can Help Foremen Improve Efficiency

There are at least three things which top management can do which will help the foreman improve the efficiency of his shop:

1. Let him have a voice in the purchase of materials, tools, and equipment: The foreman lives every day with the materials, tools, and equipment in his department. He knows the good and bad points of every brand-name in his shop. He knows which items speed up production and which ones do not. While there is no need to give the foreman the last word on purchases made for his shop, he should be given the opportunity to express his opinions on the matter. In most cases, he will be able to offer ideas that will influence the type of purchases to be made. This should result in having more efficient equipment and in improved morale of the work force.

2. Let him select his own employees: Recruiting of personnel should be done through the personnel office, based upon qualifications submitted by the foreman. But the foreman should have the authority to determine which of the applicants submitted by the personnel office he wants to have in his department. This enables the foreman to select those people whom he feels will be most capable of doing the job the way he wants it done. Such an arrangement is conducive to a more harmonious shop, and helps give the foreman the prestige necessary to carry out his responsibility. The personnel office should continue to make personnel policies to which the foreman should of course conform, but a foreman should have the freedom to select his own employees within the limit of those policies.

3. Give the foreman authority to recommend or deny wage increases: If the foreman wants to have the wage of one of his employees raised, he should have the authority to recommend the increase. Moreover, every effort should be made to grant it, provided it does not conflict with the plant's overall personnel policies. This procedure helps also to increase the prestige of the foreman and gives the workers assurance that their ability to get wage increases is not dependent solely upon some higher authority who is unfamiliar with their work. Conversely, if the worker's performance does not, in the opinion of the foreman, justify a proposed wage increase, he should be authorized to deny it. If the plant is a union shop, of course, suitable adjustments in these policies would have to be made.

III. THE FOREMAN'S TRAINING FUNCTIONS

A foreman has to assume certain training functions—whether the plant has a training department or not because there are certain procedures and techniques which are peculiar to many jobs. In a small plant, it is often difficult for anyone outside of the department in question to be entirely familiar with its procedures and techniques. Moreover, procedural changes often take place so fast that a centralized training department would find it almost impossible to keep on a current basis.

Training New Employees

The foreman has a threefold training responsibility for new employees:

1. Explaining company policies: He has a responsibility, at the time the new employee reports for work, to brief him on all company policies which directly relate to him individually; for example: regulations regarding pay, including lost time and overtime, seniority provisions, seniority increases, union contract provisions, and promotions; company-sponsored insurance plans; workmen's compensation, and the rights of the employee in connection with each. These are items of such importance to the new employee that they are an essential part of his orientation.

2. Instruction covering shop operations: The foreman also has a responsibility to introduce the new employee around the shop, explain the functions of each worker, point out the different types of equipment and what they are used for, and explain shop safety regulations. He also should explain the relationship of the new employee's job to the rest of the department and to the rest of the company, and briefly outline the organization of the company as a whole. This helps the employee to get a proper perspective of his new job and the plant.

3. Coaching covering the job of a new employee: The foreman has a responsibility to see that the new employee is properly broken in on his new job. This is usually done by assigning him to an experienced employee who provides detailed instruction and assistance until the new worker is qualified to handle his assignments alone.

When a new employee is hired for a complicated job requiring several different types of operations, foremen frequently break the job done into a series of simple steps, to facilitate training. When the new employee learns how to handle the first operation, he is then instructed on how to do the second operation until he has mastered that step, and so on. This is known as the "job dilution" type of training. It was widely used in shops both large and small during World War II. This method of breaking in a new employee on a complicated job usually accelerate the training period with a minimum of effort.

Training Employees Promoted to New Jobs

When an employee is promoted or transferred to a different job, the foreman has a responsibility to see that adequate instruction is given the worker on his new job until he is qualified to handle his assignments alone. As in the case of a newly hired employee, such training usually requires that an experienced employee provide the necessary detailed instruction.

Training an Understudy

The foreman has a responsibility to develop an understudy who can take over his job if and when he is promoted or leaves the company.

Some men hesitate to develop an understudy because they feel he may eventually prove to be a competitor for the job of foreman. Yet a foreman owes it to himself to have an understudy who can take his place. Failure to have one may prevent him from being promoted to a better job, simply because there is no one to take his place. In many cases, an oversight of this nature has stood in the way of a foreman's promotion.

From the plant manager's viewpoint, an understudy is desirable because of the possibility that the foreman may get sick, leave the company, or be eligible for transfer or promotion.

Other Training Responsibilities

Foremen are often given other types of training responsibilities, among which are the following:

1. Orientation of Salesmen and Other Company Personnel: Foremen are often called upon to explain the production process to salesmen for their information in selling the product to customers. Others in the company who hold management positions often call upon the foreman to give them the same briefing so they can get a more complete picture of plant operations. Sometimes foremen are called upon to explain the production process to customers who want to know how the product they buy is made.

2. Special Training Sessions for Employees: When major changes are made in the production process, plant mechanization is increased, wage payment systems are changed, time-study plans are introduced, plant operations are reorganized, or special sales and advertising campaigns are initiated., the foreman has a responsibility to explain to his employees the reasons why the changes are taking place, and how these changes will affect them.

Some plant, realizing that the foreman is the company so far as his employees are concerned, rely upon him to hold employee training sessions in cooperation with other supervisors for the purpose of acquainting employees with the operations of the company in general, why it operates the way it does, what the plant balance sheet shows, what the current business conditions are and how they affect the operations of the company, and what the prospects of the company are for the future. Such sessions help to educate the worker with respect to economics and the free enterprise system. Most research organizations agree that employees are in need of such training because many of them are often ill-informed on matters of this nature.

IV. THE FOREMAN'S PERSONAL RELATIONSHIPS AND CONTACTS

In the average small plant, each function and each department is so interdependent that the foreman who succeeds in establishing good personal relationships throughout the company has a much easier time performing his job. Since the foreman's shop is dependent upon other departments for materials, equipment, supplies, and personnel, the amount of cooperation he is able to get from other departments has a definite effect upon the performance of his shop.

Relationships With Workers

The value of good personal relationships between the foreman and his employees cannot be overestimated, because it is through such relationships that he is able to settle more grievances and avert more union complaints than any other member of the management team. A foreman in one small plant, for example, is known to have settled an average of one grievance a month for the past 5 years. His technique is simple. He listens until the worker gets the complaint off his chest. Then, if the worker is upset at the time the complaint is made, he waits until the next day, when the subject can be discussed more objectively. If after investigation he finds that the complaint is valid, he takes corrective action provided his department is at fault. If another department is at fault, such as the payroll or personnel office, he request the department in question to take corrective action. And he follows up on the matter until the case is closed.

If a foreman does not enjoy good personal relationships with his employees, they may not choose to discuss their grievances with him. They may, instead, take them direct to the union and thereby strain the relationship between union and plant before the matter is settled. There is evidence that good foreman-employee relationships have been responsible for smoothing out many grievances which otherwise would have resulted in strikes.

Foremen who enjoy the best personal relationships with their employees are those whose actions prove that they sincerely have the interest of their workers at heart. Such action becomes evident in the foreman's efforts to provide his employees with adequate equipment and supplies; when he tries to make the job easier for them; when he tries to improve their comfort while on the job; when he takes an interest in seeing that they get their paychecks on time and in the right amount; when he makes allowances for illness in the family or other personal difficulties of his workers; and when he tries to promote harmony among all of the people in his department.

Many foremen find that occasional parties after work help to improve morale by enabling everybody to get acquainted. Also, occasional social visits to the homes of his employees improves their job interest and enables the foreman to know them better. If a foreman operates his shop on a strictly impartial basis, visit to the home of his employees are a great help in improving morale.

Contacts With Supervisors in Other Departments

Much that is used within a shop, such as materials and supplies, comes from other departments. The foreman, therefore, has to have the cooperation of these other departments if he is to get from them the kind of service he needs in order to keep his shop running efficiently. While it is true that he can appeal to his superior if the cooperation he wants from other departments is not adequate, this procedure takes time. It creates even worse feelings, and in the long run, the foreman who made the complaint loses more than he gains. There is no substitute for good, spontaneous, interdepartmental cooperation.

Relationships With Superiors

The foreman has a responsibility to keep his superiors informed regarding his problems, his needs and the overall operations of his department. Top management relies on information of this nature for control and planning purposes. He also has a responsibility to keep his superiors currently informed regarding those problems and situations affecting the performance of his shop which are outside the scope of his authority to handle. Failure to keep his superiors properly informed may result in eventual embarrassment to the foreman because a small problem, over which he has no control, may later develop into a major problem if it is allowed to go unattended.

Contacts With Unions and Union Officials

A foreman's contacts with unions and union officials must at all times be honest and sincere. There is no other way to deal effectively with unions. It is a foreman's responsibility to respect and abide by the agreement which his company and his employees' union have developed. The foreman helps to promote better management-labor relations when the union knows that he fully respects and makes a sincere effort to support all provisions of the agreement which his company has signed.

Contacts With the Public

The foreman is often called upon to handle plant tours for groups who want to see how products are manufactured. This places a public relations responsibility upon the foreman to give such visitors a good impression of the plant. Industrial management is becoming more and more aware of the need to acquaint the general public with the facts about its plants and the contributions which they make to the community. One of the more effective ways to do this is through plant tours.

The heads of many plants encourage the foremen and other supervisors to take part as much as possible in civic activities designed to improve the community in which the plant is located. They take the position that since the plant is a part of the community, the leadership in that plant should take a definite interest in community affairs. When the foreman engages in such activities, he not only advertises his company as being a civic-minded organization, but he assumes community responsibilities which contribute to the growth of both himself and the community.

V. DEVELOPING BETTER FOREMEN

The problem of developing better foremen is more than just a matter of putting them through a foremanship training course. In fact, a training program is only one of several factors which have a bearing on the development of foremen. Before there can be effective training, it must first be determined that the foremen and prospective foremen possess the basic qualifications which such a job demands. Any time spent in training people in foremanship is wasted unless those being trained actually have the qualifications necessary to absorb and use such training effectively.

Even then, the maximum effectiveness of a foreman training program cannot be realized unless top management follows up such training with an arrangement which provides proper recognition of the role which a foreman is expected to play in his organization. If a foreman completes training course which stresses the importance of his job (and virtually all foremen training courses do stress this) and later finds that the importance of that job is minimized through lack of proper authority and recognition, part of the value of the training course is lost.

The problem of developing better foremen is, therefore, one which involves three basic considerations: (1) the prospective foreman must be qualified for the job, (2) special training for development on the job should be available, and (3) the importance of the role the foreman is expected to play in the operation of the plant should be fully recognized.

Qualifications Which Foremen Need

The wide publicity given in recent years to the importance of the role played by foremen in industry has developed a realization by top management that, in the eyes of the worker, the foreman is the company, and, in the eyes of the community, the company is judged in part by the impression the foreman makes on the general public. This realization has resulted in a more careful selection of people who are placed in such jobs. Since the foreman is charged with the responsibility of getting the job done in the quickest possible time and with the least possible expense, he must be a highly qualified person. Recent studies by management associations and research organizations generally indicate that top management today is looking for the following nine qualifications in the people who are considered for the position of foreman:

1. Leadership Ability: A recent survey taken among 300 companies indicates that leadership ability is the first qualification that top management looks for in a prospective foreman. The modern concept of a foreman is one who provides leadership, not one who simply gives orders. His ability to get production out on time with the least possible cost is dependent to a large extent upon how effectively his leadership can stimulate job interest and satisfaction on the part of his employees. A foreman is a good leader when his employees turn out a good job not because they have to but because they as employees want to do a good job.

2. Organizing Ability: A foreman has men, machines, and materials assigned to him. He must have the ability to organize all three factors in an orderly, clear-cut, and simplified manner, whenever circumstances demand it. Nothing will break down the morale of a shop quicker than a situation where the work is so poorly organized that the employees are, figuratively, stepping on each other, or where some employees are overworked while others are standing around waiting for work. Unless a foreman has the administrative skill necessary to organize the work of his shop in a manner that will hold bottlenecks and trouble spots to a minimum, his other qualifications as a foreman will be of little value.

3. Character: A foreman has to be honest and fair with his employees at all times. In this respect his reputation must be above reproach. One of the costliest operators a company can have is a foreman or supervisor who arouses suspicion and distrust. Employees will invariably produce less work under such supervision. Their morale will not only be low, but they will spend valuable production time worrying about what the foreman is going to do next. These result in rumors and secret discussions between employees on company time, which increases the time and the cost required to get out production.

4. Judgment: Employees do better work when they have confidence in the foreman's judgment. Especially is this true in a shop where poor judgment could result in accidents to employees. Very often employees are asked to do a job or follow a procedure in which they do not see any merit. Confidence in the judgment of the foreman will tend to allay any fears that the foreman doesn't know what he is doing.

5. Technical Skill and Mechanical Ability: The idea foreman should be able to run any machine in the shop as well if not better than any employee under his supervision. It helps strengthen his position as a leader. However, this is not always possible because some machines cannot be operated at peak efficiency unless a person has daily experience with them. Nevertheless, a foreman should know the capabilities and limitations of every machine in his department and should be able to tell new people how to operate them effectively.

6. Education: While it is true that more and more foremen have had college training, a college education is not regarded as a necessary qualification. Some of the country's best foremen have never been to college. Insofar as education is concerned, top management is looking, first, for foremen whose background provides a broad common sense viewpoint and practical understanding. Although college training helps in the development of these qualities, it is also recognized that such qualities can be the outgrowth of past experience.

7. Initiative: A foreman must be a self-starter. If he is to discharge his responsibility as a manager of a function, he must be capable of taking action necessary to keep production going with only occasional supervision from his superiors. Any foreman who requires constant supervision is not performing the functions of a foreman.

8. Human Interest: A foreman should be interested in all things which affect the wellbeing of his employees. This involves personal as well as shop problems because personal problems frequently affect performance on the job. Moreover, the foreman is, oftentimes, the only person to whom employees can go for counsel and advice on problems of this nature. When a worker knows that the foreman has his personal interest at heart, his morale and job interest are greatly stimulated.

9. Physical and Mental Requirements: It is needless to say that a foreman must have the physical and emotional capacity to carry his responsibilities and perform his duties with the vigor which the job requires.

Finding Prospects

Companies generally try to find people within their own organization who can be promoted to the position of foreman whenever a vacancy occurs. They do this because it has a definite bearing on the growth and development of foremen into better supervisors. When a man is promoted from the ranks to the position of foreman, he is given evidence that the company is trying to follow the policy of "promotion from within." This gives him the feeling that if he does a good job as foreman he may have a chance at some later date to be considered for an even better job. A foreman who feels he can look to his own company for advancement, rather than having to look to a competitor, is able for psychological reasons, to give more of himself to his job and his company. This procedure also helps stimulate job interest on the part of the foreman's employees because they too feel that if they do a good job where they are, they may later be advanced to the position of foreman. More and more employees are looking for jobs that offer career opportunities, and as long as a company holds to the policy of promotion from within, workers can feel that their present company offers career possibilities.

What Kind of Training?

Programs for training foremen take various forms. Among them are: programs designed to prepare candidates for promotion to the job of a foreman; programs designed to stimulate die development of existing foremen so they can do a better job; refresher courses for foremen who have already been trained; and programs designed to train foremen for higher positions in the organization.

The fact that foreman training is so strongly emphasized by industry does not mean that the foreman of today is lacking in capability. On the contrary, most foremen are capable, well-qualified people. However, attitudes of people are constantly changing, new labor relations philosophies are being developed, and new processes and new techniques are being introduced. It is only good business to expose foremen to training sessions which will give them the information necessary to keep abreast of the changing industrial picture. The primary reason why such careful attention has been given to the subject of foremen training in recent years is the long-unfilled need which resulted from the time when it was not felt necessary to train foremen at all. It was felt that this need could be adequately met through supervision of the foreman by his superiors. Here is another example of the fact that industrial philosophies and practices change.

A foreman on the job today already has a certain amount of leadership ability, organizational ability, understanding of people, technical skill, and mechanical ability. These are qualifications he has to possess if he is to hold down his job. He can't get production out on time without them. The question is: Can the foreman's ability to lead and understand people, and organize his shop, be improved with training designed to help him in these areas? The answer is: "Yes." Leaders from both large and small companies agree that training in foremanship can definitely help the foreman to develop his abilities and thereby enable him to do a better job in the plant. In addition, after a foreman has taken a course in leadership training, he needs refresher courses from time to time because under pressure of meeting schedules and deadlines even the most conscientious supervisor forgets or overlooks part of what he already knows. Experience proves that die art of getting things done through people is a subject which supervisors can, with profit, be coached in—at regular intervals.

The foreman also needs training in shop organization and in work simplification. There are certain basic principles of good organization which can be applied to most any department. Also, new techniques are developed from time to time which permit plant procedures to be simplified with a saving of time and money. Any foreman training program should deal with the subject of shop organization techniques because good organization reduces waste and production costs and improves employee morale.

Solving the Problem in Small Plants

Because of practical considerations, small plants are limited in their ability to develop and promote their own formal training programs for foremen. Nevertheless, many of them consider the need for this training to be of such importance that they are discovering ways and means for making it available in spite of limited resources. In general, small plants are working through one of four general methods.

1. Cooperation With Other Small Plants: In areas where a number of small plants are located, arrangement can often be made whereby several plants jointly hire a training specialist who develops a foreman training program designed to fit the particular needs of the cooperating plants. Such projects are financed by the cooperating firms on a joint basis. Arrangements of this type have proved successful in Chicago, Pittsburgh, and Philadelphia. The idea was developed with the help of management consulting firms.

2. Cooperation With Colleges and Universities: Some colleges and universities, in cooperation with small plants, have developed foreman and supervisory training programs designed to meet the needs of plants in their particular areas. These programs are usually offered in connection with adult training courses given by the colleges. Those who attend usually get the benefit of instruction both from college professors who have specialized in training problems and from industrial experts. While there are relatively few such arrangement—at least so far as foremen are concerned—plants that have participated in projects of this type regard them as most successful. An alternative method of training foreman is the home study course. Subjects taught by accredited home study schools include quality control, report writing, safety engineering, and others.

3. Use of Programs Developed By Larger Companies: Some small plants purchase foreman training programs from larger companies which are in the same general type of business. They use such programs to conduct training sessions under the

leadership of someone on their own staff. Some large companies are very generous in letting other companies use their material. While this arrangement has its disadvantages, it has been known to produce desirable results, especially where the directors of such training sessions are skilled in conference leadership techniques. Those who use this arrangement point out that, in the final analysis, foremen will train each other if (a) they have an adequate text upon which to base their discussions, and (b) the leader of the training sessions is gifted in stimulating group discussions in connection with problems which foreman as individuals face on their particular jobs.

Where a small company has a close relationship with one of the larger companies, arrangements can often be made whereby the small plant sends a member of its staff to attend the foreman training course of the large company. That person ultimately returns and serves as an instructor for foremen in his own plant. It should be noted, however, that training programs developed for large companies need to be modified if they are used in small plants.

4. Use of Supervisory Programs Developed By Management Associations: Some small plants solve their foreman training problem by making use of the staff facilities of national management associations. The assistance rendered by such organizations to small plants has produced excellent results. Among those associations which have taken an active interest in foremen training are the National Association of Manufacturers, some local Chambers of Commerce, the National Association of Foremen, the Foremen's League, and the American Management Association. These groups offer a variety of services which can and are being utilized by small companies as follows:

   a. Some have training specialists who are available to small businesses for the purpose of conducting foremen and supervisory training programs.
   b. Some have training specialists available as consultants of the purpose of helping small establishments set up their own training program.
   c. Some have foreman training programs of various types which small plants can use in conducting their own training sessions.
   d. Some offer a generalize type of foreman training through the use of foremen's clubs. Such clubs are designed to promote a better understanding by the foreman of his responsibilities as a member of management.

Measuring the Results

Since a training program for foremen deals with leadership and organizational problems, the results of the training can usually be measured only in terms of the foreman's performance on the job. There is no way to predict from classroom discussions how valuable the training will be to the company. The results of such training, if they are to be of value, must be reflected in the performance records of the foreman's department. If the course has been a success, proof will be found in increased ability to get work out in less time, with less expense, and with fewer employee grievances than previously. While it may take weeks for any results to become apparent, a good foreman training program will help to accomplish this objective. Following are the specific items by which the foreman's performance can be measured to determine what results have been obtained: overtime expense, number of production units which have been rejected, amount of material wasted, number of workers required to get the work out, number of hours the machines are utilized, the number and nature of employee grievances which are filed, and the amount of absenteeism. If the training program has been successful, there should in due time be an improvement in each of the categories listed above.

How Top Management Promotes Foreman Development

A training program alone is not sufficient to encourage the development of foremen to the maximum extent. After a foreman has completed his training, he wants to see evidence that his job is as important as the training program led him to believe. If he is to be regarded as a part of management, he wants to be given the authority, prestige, and recognition which goes with it. Once he has been given proper recognition, this tends to serve as a constant reminder of the importance of his job and encourages him to make greater efforts toward self-improvement on his own initiative.

There are several ways in which top management can provide the proper recognition to foremen:

1. Incentive Payments: Many firms have the policy of paying bonuses to their top management in proportion to their salaries, based upon how much profit the company makes each year. By spreading such bonus payments to all levels of management, foremen and other supervisors are made to feel that they really are a part of management and that the more efficiently they run their shops, the greater the chance that their annual bonuses will be increased.

2. Authority: It is not enough to spell out the duties and responsibilities of the foreman. He must be given suitable authority. Top management should also make it clear that they will back up the foreman in any decisions that he makes within the scope of his duties and responsibilities. This helps to promote the growth of the foreman because it keeps him alert to the fact that he is, in reality as well as title, a part of management.

3. Prestige: Top management can develop a sense of responsibility and job satisfaction in its foremen, by use of the following other devices:

    a. A bulletin from the president to all levels of management informing them of any major changes in company policy. It lets the foreman and other supervisors know that the top management prefers for supervisors to get the story direct rather than through the grapevine or the newspapers.

    b. Staff sessions called by top management of a small plant for the purpose of getting advice on company problems have proved effective in developing a broader sense of responsibility among foremen.

    c. Occasional banquet where all levels of management are invited for getting-acquainted purposes helps to stimulate job enthusiasm on the part of foremen.

A foreman who is properly trained and who enjoys proper recognition of his status is one of the most important people in industry today. The extent to which he develops his abilities to do the job expected of him is, in large measure, dependent upon how much interest top management in the small plant is willing to take in him.